ADVOCACY SKILLS:
A HANDBOOK FOR HUMAN SERVICE
PROFESSIONALS

D0890394

For Julie, Jessica, Caitlin and Calum

Advocacy Skills:
A Handbook for Human
Service Professionals

Neil Bateman

© Neil Bateman 1995

All rights reserved. No part of this publication may be reproduced, stored in a retrieval system, or transmitted in any form or by any means, electronic, mechanical, photocopying, recording or otherwise without the prior permission of the publisher.

Published by
Arena
Ashgate Publishing Limited
Gower House
Croft Road
Aldershot
Hants GU11 3HR
England

Ashgate Publishing Company
Old Post Road
Brookfield
Vermont 05036
USA

British Library Cataloguing in Publication Data

Bateman, Neil.
  Advocacy Skills: Handbook for Human
  Service Professionals
  I. Title
  344.20752
ISBN 1–85742–200–7

Library of Congress Cataloging-in-Publication Data

Bateman, Neil, 1955–
  Advocacy skills: a handbook for human service
  professionals / Neil Bateman
      p.   cm.
  Includes bibliographical references and index.
  ISBN 1–85742–200–7 (pbk): $24.95 (approx.)
  1. Social advocacy.   2. Human services – Philosophy.
  3. Human services – Methodology.   4. Social services –
  Methodology. I. Title.
  HV31.B28 1995
  381–dc 20

94–24121
CIP

Typeset in 10pt Palatino by Raven Typesetters, Chester
Printed in Great Britain by Hartnolls Ltd, Bodmin

Contents

Preface

Advocacy often involves challenging accepted norms and rules that restrict people's lives. By demonstrating the skills of advocacy, this book aims, primarily, to help individuals working in welfare organisations become effective advocates on behalf of other people.

Who this book is for

Many people working in different settings act as advocates. They might be doctors, social workers, nurses, advice workers, members of the clergy, people working in the education system or housing officials. They may also be trade union officials who act as advocates for their members. This book is aimed at them, and not at lawyers. Lawyers need more specialist texts to take account of the type of advocacy they undertake, but some of the chapters, including those on negotiation and interviewing, might still be useful for them. For simplicity, I describe people who undertake advocacy as 'advocates'.

What this book explains

Successful advocacy is satisfying, unsuccessful advocacy is not satisfying. You can become a better advocate by adopting the approach discussed in this book. Through becoming a better advocate with more successes, your job will be more enjoyable and your clients will be happier.

Advocacy is often assumed to be a skill that one either has or hasn't. This is not so; advocacy is a skill as much as any other method of helping people is a skill. Many believe that the key to effective advocacy lies in having good technical knowledge. While good knowledge is essential and can boost one's confidence, its pursuit can displace advocacy as a skill in itself, thus preventing many people from thinking that they are capable of acting as an advocate. You do not need to have several years' technical or legal training to be an effective advocate – this book shows that. This book is about a skill that ordinary people, doing ordinary jobs helping others, use every day, and is part of helping others achieve their full potential. Advocacy can set wrongs to rights and is at the heart of the helping process. Advocacy can empower the powerless and gives people a voice. Advocacy is caring about injustice.

Indeed, advocacy is the reason why many people choose to work in the helping professions. Caring about the way people are treated and feeling that you can do something to help is why most of us decided to take on such jobs. Credible professionals are prepared to raise uncomfortable issues and to highlight where things are wrong. Failure to do so is to retreat into the safe haven of bureaucracy, and few people choose to work in the welfare state because they want to be bureaucrats!

All manner of welfare professionals engage in advocacy – and they enjoy it because it can furnish one of those rare moments in their working lives when they feel they have helped someone. Housing officers will argue with their superiors about why a family should be rehoused; social workers will push for someone to get extra help, and nurses will argue with hospital accountants and doctors that, despite the cost, a patient should get particular treatment. Effective benefit officials will look for a favourable legal interpretation to get extra benefit for a claimant – even if their manager tells them not to.

Advocacy is not easy – it involves you in extra work and you may meet resistance. But it may also save you extra work in the long run. Advocacy can also involve looking at complex issues of fact and law that may have to go to court or which go to the heart of someone's treatment of another person. It is hardly surprising that advocacy is controversial. The effective advocate may well be challenging accepted practice and disrupting cosy professional relationships. The advocate is likely to be acting on behalf of people who are not universally popular. People who use public welfare services are often poor and marginalised. They may be homeless, they may exhibit unusual behaviour, and may have criminal records. They may abuse others and themselves. These are not the traits associated with success in society, and advocates who support such people may themselves be marginalised solely through guilt by association – even by the organisation that is charged with helping such individuals.

Advocacy is viewed with ambiguity by many welfare organisations. On the one hand, health and social services bodies may give funding to service users to run advocacy groups, but those at the top of such bodies will have private (and not so private) fears about the group being too effective.

Welfare organisations may recruit individual staff and agree that they can advocate on behalf of individuals but, if that advocacy is thorough and strong, their enthusiasm for such actions can diminish.

Some local authorities will fund law centres – if they do not do more than gently nibble the hand that feeds. Indeed, there are many recorded instances of individuals and groups engaged in advocacy having their funding withdrawn. Redundancy is far from unknown among advocates employed in the welfare state. In extreme cases, individual advocates can face disciplinary sanctions for engaging in advocacy.

How far a society is able to tolerate and encourage advocacy is a test of that society's commitment to democracy and pluralism. It is also a test of how seriously it takes the notion that dispossessed members of society have rights that must be upheld if those rights are to have any meaning. If rights are enshrined in law, it would be sheer dishonesty if people were unable to seek to enforce them.

Advocacy thus raises fundamental questions about the nature of a society, its constitution and its respect for individuals. The greater the furtherance of advocacy the healthier that society is. A society that jealously safeguards and protects its vulnerable members is likely to be a more tolerant, pleasanter place, and it is likely to be a society that thrives on new ideas and activities: in short, the type of society in which most people who work for welfare organisations wish to live.

How to use this book

I have deliberately avoided a weighty, theoretical approach. This is for two main reasons.

First, there is very little published material about advocacy skills. There are several books on advocacy for lawyers, but these are of little use to people employed in human service organisations. Advocacy as a skill for welfare professionals is a comparatively recent development so, over time, concepts and different approaches to advocacy will crystallise and thence a body of theoretical knowledge will form. That crystallisation has not yet occurred.

Second, advocacy is a very practical skill. It must be developed by practice, and the subtleties associated with other helping skills are often not relevant. If you have read this far you will be serious about developing your advocacy skills and will want to know how to be a better advocate.

You should aim to read the whole book. As most readers will not read the book at one sitting, each chapter covers a separate issue. At the end of each chapter, your understanding of advocacy will be better and you should have a grasp of a particular aspect of advocacy skills. You will notice that the main chapters on the practice of advocacy contain exercises, standard letters and case-studies. Please don't ignore these. Not only are these exercises useful in themselves, but they demonstrate the techniques discussed in that chapter.

You should also try to read the book in the order it is written, and avoid skipping chapters. Effective advocacy must have a structure and, because advocacy takes place over a period of time, it is sequential in nature. The structure of the book reflects this. As is explained later, advocacy can be ineffective if its sequential nature is ignored. Skip chapters at your peril!

If I succeed in laying out a theoretical framework for others to develop and debate, and if I have helped others become better advocates, the effort involved in writing this book will have been worthwhile.

Any legal references are correct as at August 1994. If subsequent changes to the law occur, the techniques described will still be valid even though the legal context may change.

Acknowledgements

Anything committed to paper is a reflection of countless experiences and ideas. Many people, some of whose names I have forgotten or never knew, inspired me to produce a book to help others become effective advocates.

However, there are some people who have been particularly influential. Among these I must mention Geoff Brogden, Andrew Brewer and Nigel Godfrey for helping me understand what advocacy can be, and Martin Davies for bringing clarity to my ideas. My colleagues at Suffolk County Council should also be acknowledged for the support they have shown in enabling me to challenge injustices.

Similarly, in the best tradition of good publishers, Jo Gooderham and others at Arena gave encouragement and support.

However, none of this would have been possible without those clients who over the years have had faith in me as an advocate.

Part I

Background

The first part of this book looks at the context of advocacy and how it can be used to secure better services, money and housing – often when such things have been refused with some force – and discusses the ethical basis of advocacy.

1 What is advocacy and why do we use it?

Definitions

It helps to be clear about what we mean by 'advocacy', as there is much debate about the meaning of the term. Such a debate – with the consequent lack of universal agreement – is inevitable given the recent and controversial history of advocacy in the helping professions.

The difficulties associated with agreeing a definition also arise where different models of advocacy develop in the welfare state. As a result, the word 'advocacy' means different things to different people. A lawyer will think of advocacy as the art of speaking in court and examining witnesses, and it may be narrowed down further to the extent that legal advocacy is claimed as the primary preserve of barristers rather than solicitors. This type of advocacy has been described as 'a standing invitation to be clever at someone else's expense'.[1] Consequently, books on advocacy for lawyers will concentrate on the combination of professional duties, legal rules and human skills involved in court-room work.

Social workers and health professionals can also act as advocates. Some, such as social workers, will have a clear responsibility to act as advocates for their clients. For others, advocacy arises as an inevitable consequence of their work with people who are disadvantaged in some way. A doctor or a nurse could be motivated by a sense of injustice or concern for the medical effects on a patient's health to write to a landlord about the patient's housing conditions or to try to persuade colleagues that a particular course of treatment is needed. This is advocacy, but it may not be recognised as such by those involved and is likely to be regarded as marginal to the main task of a medical practitioner. Even so, the improvement in housing and health that may follow such actions could be more effective than anything available on prescription.

1

A voluntary body may want to challenge a statement of special educational needs for a child. A housing official may be motivated by a combined need to improve their employer's cashflow and concern for the affected individual when taking up a case of late payment of benefit to a local authority tenant. Similarly, a social worker may want to obtain extra money or a particular service for a client for several reasons. Advocacy will be used as the means to do so, although it may not be thought of as being advocacy.

In the last few years the influence of Citizen Advocacy has been profound. Developed in The Netherlands and the United States, Citizen Advocacy has formed a distinct identity and provided credibility for the idea that service users have rights in the way that professionals treat them.

Often Citizen Advocacy concentrates upon the way that services are provided by and in institutions. This reflects the fact that Citizen Advocacy first developed as a way of helping people with learning disabilities to influence the services they receive.

The advocate engaged in Citizen Advocacy may be concerned with an apparently mundane matter – for example, the choice of clothing for a person with a learning disability. However, such matters are of inestimable importance to those whose appearance is decided by others. Parents and institutions may have oppressive and outdated views on what clothes should be imposed on a person with learning disabilities. Citizen Advocates try to help that person express their wishes, thus helping them to become full citizens.

It is already clear that different people will be engaged in different forms of advocacy: from the quasi-legal to the very personal. There is, however, a set of core skills that is common to all forms of advocacy. In addition, the tasks that the advocates undertake have a common theme – helping another person obtain something from someone with power. Sometimes what is being sought is clear and structured – for example, extra social security benefits governed by legal rules; at other times it is unstructured and without clear boundaries. The work of Citizen Advocates and nurses is often concerned with the latter situation. One could characterise advocacy on the first type of problem as 'hard' advocacy and as 'soft' advocacy on the latter type. Whatever the type of problem, the *advocacy* must be structured if it is to be effective.

Dictionaries can help us define what we mean by advocacy. The *Concise Oxford Dictionary* defines advocacy as '. . . function of an advocate, pleading in support . . .' It is perhaps obvious that advocacy is the function of an advocate. It is sometimes unclear that, while undertaking advocacy, one acts as an advocate for the service user. There is a clear instructional relationship. The second part of this dictionary definition takes us further. 'Pleading' is meant in the sense of reasoned argument rather than pleading for mercy. This is the way that lawyers construe advocacy. Such a definition is consistent with the 'softer' forms of advocacy on unstructured problems.

The *Concise Oxford Dictionary*'s definition of 'advocate' is also interesting. It reads: '. . . one who pleads for another, one who speaks in favour of . . .' Clearly this implies that advocacy involves arguing on behalf of another rather than on one's own behalf. Indeed, there are many successful advocates who readily admit that they make poor self-advocates. Perhaps the inevitable subjectivity and self-doubt undermines one's efforts. At the most extreme, it is interesting that solicitors charged with criminal or professional offences usually employ another lawyer to act for them.

Another definition in the *Concise Oxford Dictionary* is of the verb 'to advocate': '. . . plead for, defend, recommend, support . . .' Advocacy is thus a positive statement: the advocate's role is to argue positively on behalf of another.

Chambers English Dictionary has similar definitions. 'Advocate' is defined as '. . . an intercessor or defender; one who pleads the cause of another . . . one who recommends or urges something'. Again the theme emerges of the advocate being someone who acts positively on behalf of someone else. This raises a number of interesting ethical issues which will be discussed later. One common definition which is not in the dictionary is 'to advocate' in the sense of 'to give voice to'; the difficulty with this definition is that it assumes that there is no need for advocacy when a person is able to voice their own concerns.

The examples given earlier show how many people working in different jobs in health, housing and social services settings can find themselves acting as advocates, and the situations described are entirely consistent with dictionary definitions of advocacy.

There are other definitions that are important in advocacy. These include:

- Client
- The other side
- Negotiation

The first two are examined in Chapter 2. Negotiation is discussed in Chapter 7.

Different approaches to advocacy

The different approaches to advocacy partly reflect the different historical roots of various professional groups within the welfare state as well as the different roles played by these groups. They are also a reflection of the differing demands of clients. Doctors will obviously advocate about medically related matters, whereas social workers will cover a broader spectrum of issues, thus reflecting the range of people and situations they address.

The mental health charity MIND has helpfully identified three main forms of advocacy.[2] These are:

- Self-advocacy
- Citizen Advocacy
- Legal advocacy

Self-advocacy

'Self-advocacy' is defined as 'a process in which an individual, or a group of people, speak or act on their own behalf in pursuit of their own needs and interests'. All of us are self-advocates to a greater or lesser extent. We go into shops and ask for particular products; we ask our manager to arrange a training course; we make our desires known daily in a variety of situations.

These are the most mundane forms of advocacy and, important as they may be for people's ability to survive in modern society, one may question whether such actions are consistent with the definitions of advocacy discussed above.

There are, however, many interesting examples of self-advocacy undertaken on a collective basis where the sum of the whole becomes greater than the sum of the individual parts – tenants' groups that organise collectively to take action on housing conditions; homeless families who act collectively to challenge the actions of housing officials; parents of children in care who form a group to support and act with other parents to challenge the actions of social services departments, and trade unions at grass roots level where members take collective action to secure improvements in pay and conditions.

Indeed, it is easy to underestimate the influence which the collective power of groups of otherwise voiceless people can have on the welfare state, and some in senior positions may try to encourage this by portraying it as a market-based concept of 'customer needs'.

Trade unions were influential in formulating proposals for a comprehensive welfare system in the 1940s. Contemporary accounts of the popular acclaim surrounding the publication of the Beveridge Report[3] in December 1942 show how there was genuine, deep public and cross-party support for such ideas, which developed from the collective notions that took hold in the wider population during the Second World War. Collectivism has been much undermined, but its roots still penetrate the far reaches of the British national psyche.

In the mid-1970s, Liverpool council tenants in a badly built block of flats colloquially known as 'The Piggeries' organised themselves with the aim of having the slum demolished. Not only did they protest but they mobilised radical lawyers to challenge the council on housing law. The result was that 'The Piggeries' were emptied, the tenants rehoused, and they established useful caselaw for use by other tenants.

Such actions have much in common with the actions of the civil rights movement in the United States in the 1960s. Indeed, groups of aggrieved individuals world-wide have achieved much by collective self-advocacy where they have integrated legal action with popular dissent.

Another example concerns the actions of the Anti-Poll Tax Union, which took much of the credit for showing how unworkable the Community Charge was by a combination of mass action and legal advocacy. Rigorous examination in Magistrates' Courts of council attempts to recover unpaid local taxes led to many embarrassments for officials as advocates – many of them unpaid and amateur – unpicked the mystical legislation during court hearings. At the same time, council meetings were picketed and demonstrations held to give a popular momentum to the organisation.

In the Third World, the clergy have taken much of the lead in developing collective self-advocacy. Synthesising populist methods of organisation and Liberation Theology, landless peasants in Central and South America have formed a bulwark against those countries, such as Guatemala, where the military has enormous political and economic power. Traditional crafts have been able to survive and indigenous culture and language have been preserved by enabling voiceless groups to assert themselves. However, this has not been without costs – witness the well-documented human rights abuses carried out when indigenous people in southern America have acted collectively.

In the welfare state, the best-known collective self-advocacy has occurred among people using mental health services and some groups of people with learning disabilities. There has also been considerable development of advocacy among people with physical disabilities.

An interesting example of collective self-advocacy is the Nottingham-based Advocacy in Action group.[4] This organisation is made up of people with learning disabilities and non-disabled co-workers. They work as a collective and actively challenge practices that restrict the lifestyles of people with learning disabilities or which take advantage of them. Advocacy in Action places a strong emphasis on learning assertiveness skills and helping members to formulate their complaints and press them home. Issues which have been tackled include a wide range of service problems – for example, lodgings where people have been treated inappropriately by the landlord. They also publish a magazine which involves people with learning disabilities in every stage of production, and which acts as an organ for their campaigning.

MIND itself has its roots in self-advocacy by people who had experience of conditions in mental hospitals. As MIND became part of the bureaucracy associated with mental health provision, its historical place has been taken by newer groups such as Survivors Speak Out. This process of self-advocacy organisations becoming part of the establishment is not new and there are many examples: tenants' associations which start out campaigning for better conditions but end up consulting with the council about evicting unpopular neighbours; disability groups which begin life campaigning about legal and institutional discrimination but themselves become providers of social services, with their users in turn complaining about *their* practices.

Many organisations find that, as their original ideas gain acceptance and the organisation is perceived as effective and representative, both the organisation and its leaders are absorbed into the very infrastructure they set out to criticise. This process is critical, and members of groups need to recognise when, rather than functioning as a campaigning self-advocacy group, they are becoming part of the problem. The turning-point appears to be when the group is given the opportunity to be institutionally effective and to co-exist with former adversaries.

The significance of self-advocacy for human service professionals is that it provides a route from which new ideas and challenges can emerge. It is also apparent that the most effective forms of self-advocacy are those where individuals act collectively and synthesise legal action with non-legal activity. Essentially, the groups and their members will be adopting a structured approach to their advocacy although they may not realise that this is the case.

Self-advocacy also implies that it is those directly affected by the problem – the sufferers of injustice, the clients, the service users – who act as advocates, but experience suggests that they often involve professional organisers, and all groups may produce informal leaders and tyrants. Professionals not directly affected by the problem can play a significant role in such groups. For example, the Towerwatch organisation in London, formed to take action about poor service delivery by the Department of Social Security Benefits Agency in the 1990s, drew its membership from both claimants and local authority welfare rights staff. Many carers' groups can point to important developmental work by people employed within helping organisations. Indeed, human service professionals have often deliberately assisted with forming self-advocacy groups to challenge their own organisations and to give a voice to their own concerns about services. This could be viewed either as cynical manipulation by middle-class individuals or as a genuine attempt to create change in partnership with those directly affected. It is a tribute to the pluralist values of the welfare state that such actions can and do occur.

Professionals involved in a group may try to limit the advocacy undertaken by the group's members so that the group may gain acceptance from the main service providers on the other side. Some individual service users within the organisation may also do the same. This may be a feature of the group entering the transitional stage of becoming a service provider itself. The current emphasis on user participation, which is partially enshrined in legislation, adds an impetus to this process, though how far self-advocacy groups are able to maintain their independence in such partnerships is debatable. The vagueness of the terms of the legislation allowing for user involvement is perhaps indicative of the transitional state of user participation.

Lindow stresses the importance of adequate funding for self-advocacy groups and that:

> in some cases, failures are caused by hope triumphing over experience. Centuries of ill-treatment and ignoring people deemed 'mad' are forgotten in a wave of goodwill. People do not realise the extent of change needed to facilitate self-advocacy – it is assumed that the statement 'You now have permission to speak' will bring forth self-advocacy.[5]

Self-advocacy groups need the same level of resources as any other area of activity. Money is needed to pay travelling expenses, training, and secretarial support. Above all, professionals involved in helping such groups must offer a genuine listening voice that does not psychoanalyse into oblivion the fears and ideas of the customer or view them as tokenist.

Self-advocacy groups must be distinct from individuals and groups that claim to act specifically for others, and the majority of the membership should consist of service users. Another feature is that self-advocacy groups often have relatively few formal structures (which is perhaps a weakness), and there will be a large element of participative democracy in their running. Groups claiming to be self-advocacy organisations which lack such features may be in transition to becoming service providers, or may just be groups of concerned individuals with limited personal experience of the issues they claim to espouse.

Features of self-advocacy

- Synthesises legal and popular action
- Often associated with a collective style of organising
- A large majority of the membership of organisations consists of those who stand to gain directly from resolution of the grievances being pursued
- May have outside input from associated professionals who wish to work in partnership
- Organisations exhibit a large element of participatory democracy and limited formal structures
- Organisations may be absorbed into the mainstream of service provision
- Debates will occur about the ethical principles of the limits and style of the advocacy and about the structure of the organisations

---

Citizen Advocacy

Despite its inception in 1966 in the United States, Citizen Advocacy is relatively underdeveloped in the United Kingdom, so there are various definitions of it. It is perhaps useful to think of Citizen Advocacy as a synthesis of advocacy and befriending; this reflects its development, which has primarily been in the context of people with learning disabilities or other disabilities which inhibit their ability to communicate effectively, and the fact that the emphasis in Citizen Advocacy lies in 'giving a voice'. Citizen Advocacy sees the advocate and service user acting in partnership – indeed, the advocate and client are described as 'partners', thus formalising an instructional relationship between them:

> Citizen advocacy occurs when an ordinary citizen develops a relationship with another person who risks social exclusion or other unfair treatment because of illness or handicap. As the relationship develops the advocate chooses to understand, respond to and represent the other person's interests as if they were the advocate's own.[6]

> The one-to-one relationship of advocate and partner is central to Citizen Advocacy and enables the advocate to use their time and energies in improving the life of a particular individual. It also provides a strong counter-balance to the general tendency of services to view people with learning disabilities as a homogeneous group rather than as individual beings with their own particular likes and dislikes.[7]

Citizen Advocates will do many everyday things such as going to social events, giving help with difficult personal issues, helping a couple get married despite opposition from people working in services, pushing for an elderly woman to receive ophthalmic treatment after waiting years for an operation, etc. They will also represent people at case conferences and meetings, help people claim benefits, and help them move to independent living. They might press for improvements in services, such as redecorating a day centre, or expose poor practice – this is perhaps a much underused aspect given the scandalous treatment in some long-stay institutions.

Citizen Advocacy has developed slowly in Europe, and is better developed in The Netherlands and Scandinavia than in the United Kingdom. One reason for the slow development of Citizen Advocacy is because funding for advocacy schemes has mostly been from public channels. There is anecdotal evidence that some senior health and local government staff who control funding have been wary of encouraging vigorous Citizen Advocacy: too many awkward questions can be asked and existing practices challenged. Another reason is that advocacy as a skill is not well recognised. There is no consensus about its definition and, culturally, north-western Europeans are often reluctant to engage in conflict – an inevitable corollary of any advocacy. Citizen Advocates have thus often concentrated upon 'softer' issues such as treatment by professionals in positions of power over the service user.

Citizen Advocacy also suffers from a fundamental weakness. The model involves the advocate acting in a variety of roles, and the different skills needed for such roles are poorly defined. By expecting a Citizen Advocate to be a friend, counsellor, legal adviser and general dogsbody, too much is placed upon the shoulders of most people. This, allied to the long-term commitment required, means that Citizen Advocacy is hard to sustain and harder to focus on the issues that matter to a service user. Research by the Bristol Advocacy Project confirms this pattern.[8] It shows that Citizen Advocates feel undermined by conflict and personalisation of issues. The study also indicated that services seem slow to respond to Citizen Advocates and sometimes want them to co-operate in dubious attempts to modify their partners' behaviour. Advocates also worried that taking action about matters – especially concerns about abuse in institutions – might rebound on their partners. Simons concluded that 'services have yet to come to terms with the direct involvement of "outsiders" of any kind (including families). If people are really going to be part of the community (as opposed to simply in it) services must become more outward looking.'[9]

In the UK the Disabled Persons Act 1986 gives people with any form of disability a legal right to have a representative. When this legislation is fully enacted and adequately resourced, it will give Citizen (and other) Advocacy a boost. However, there are concerns about the cost of advocates. It has been estimated that to cater for the 144 000 people who are likely to need advocates at an average cost of £215 each per year, nearly £31 million would have to be allocated.[10] The activities of effective advocates would also have the effect of increasing pressure on public spending as shortfalls in service provision were identified and successfully challenged.

Citizen Advocates are:

- Independent from the organisation providing the service, and free of conflicts of interest
- Not relatives of the client/partner
- Willing, committed members of the community who try to secure individuals' rights as well as act as companions and helpers
- Prepared to enter into a long-term, sustained, helping relationship with the client/partner

Legal advocacy

Advocacy has always been claimed as the forte of lawyers. This is particularly so of barristers, who have a virtual legal monopoly on appearances in many courts. Lawyers view advocacy as the act of representing clients before courts and tribunals.

I draw several distinctions between advocacy in human service professions and that undertaken by lawyers. First, in human service professions, advocacy will usually take place outside the court-room; much effective work is undertaken by letter or on the phone. Second, the skills and ethics of advocacy in the court-room can apply equally outside court and should be used by all advocates. For example: 'The task of the advocate is to be argumentative, inquisitive, indignant or apologetic – as the occasion demands – and always persuasive on behalf of the person who pays for his voice.'[11] Third, most human service professionals are not paid by their clients – they usually don't have the funds to pay even if the practice of charging were to be developed. Fourth, legal advocacy may involve complex points of law and require considerable legal training. While advocacy by human service professionals would benefit from the correct application of legal principles, and while it is essential to use the law in all advocacy, effective advocacy on many matters can be undertaken by people without legal training.

The apparent complexity of legal matters excludes many people from enforcing their rights. One of the features of our legal system is that it is rooted in historical principles, uses much archaic language and its proponents dress in old-fashioned clothing. All of this creates (perhaps unwittingly) an aura of remoteness from everyday life and everyday people with everyday problems. Is it any wonder that judges ask barristers to explain 'Who is Gazza? Is he a rugby or association football player?' In such a culture, the mystique and strict rules requiring legal advocates to have a long training not only exclude many working-class people from entry to the law but reinforce the mistaken belief that legal training is essential for the resolution of even the simplest problems. All of this produces rich pickings for the legal profession.

The skills of legal advocacy can be effectively transferred to human services and used by them, and the skills involved have much to offer when pursuing people's rights. However, it is necessary to recognise one's limitations and to use legal advocates where necessary. One must recognise that great improvements to the rights of poor people have been made as a direct result of work by legal advocates: in particular, the rights of homeless people have been usefully clarified and improved by the work of lawyers acting as advocates. But one must also be aware that most lawyers do not have the necessary skills and experience to act as effective advocates in the areas that many users of welfare services require, and that the limitations of the Legal Aid scheme often mean that, even if the right legal help is available, the money to pay for it isn't. Furthermore, effective legal advocacy also requires good inter-personal skills and creativity. These may be lacking in a lawyer whose training concentrated upon traditional legal skills. Even so, there may come a point when particular legal expertise and skill is required to resolve problems. This is when the lawyer or specialist adviser should be used.

Legal advocacy

- Usually based upon a contractual or financial relationship
- The nature of the problem may involve advocacy which becomes remote from the client
- Difficult for most people to engage in because of complex rules of conduct and limited rights of audience before courts
- Not concerned with the non-legal aspects of advocacy
- Highly effective when used to push back the boundaries of legal understanding of people's rights

---

But to redress the balance, the inception of formal appeal tribunals on special education needs may provide scope for synthesising a range of skills when acting as an advocate on such matters. On the other hand, there is a synthesis which has proved itself over the years . . .

The welfare rights movement

The origins of the welfare rights movement lie in the synthesis of Quakerism and the United States' civil rights movement. In the 1960s it became apparent to many people that the post-war welfare states had not eradicated poverty and that there was massive discrimination and flouting of legal safeguards within the income maintenance systems. The civil rights movement drew in radical lawyers and advisers to mount legal challenges to racism in the US income maintenance (or 'welfare') systems administered by various states. Because of the level of poverty among black people, the civil rights movement used legal challenges as part of their political campaigning.

In the UK in the late 1960s the then Labour government initiated the Community Development Projects. These schemes were designed to help stimulate local activity in areas of social deprivation. By this time the welfare rights movement had formed an identity, and tangible gains from advocacy on income maintenance issues were clear to those affected. At the same time, the Child Poverty Action Group (CPAG) was founded by academics and Quakers who were concerned at the persistence of poverty in the UK. In the same era, Shelter, the national campaign for homeless people, was founded to campaign for improved housing and to stimulate the provision of advice about housing rights.

CPAG began to offer an advice facility for the public and those working in the welfare state. They also undertook a deliberate strategy of pursuing test cases on social security matters both to publicise the obvious injustices in the system and to secure improvements to it. Indeed, one of their earliest publications was a booklet entitled *Test Cases for the Poor*. Another publication, that has now become a classic, was the *National Welfare Benefits Handbook*. The aim of this book was to empower benefit claimants and their advisers. (Do remember that, at this time, even the official government guidance on social security matters was covered by the Official Secrets Act.)

In 1968 Oxfordshire County Council appointed the first ever welfare rights officer. This represented a watershed because it had become recognised (in some quarters at least) that advocacy on social security matters was a skill that was relevant and helpful for those working in the personal social services. Formal advocacy – including advocacy before tribunals – was starting to be viewed as a model of intervention that depersonalised individuals' hardships and challenged wider notions of inequality. It also obtained money for people when the system had refused it, and could make a major impact on the lives of individual poor people.

In the late 1970s and early 1980s there was a massive growth of welfare rights units within local authorities. Often starting with just one or two staff and then growing rapidly as their work became politically popular, the movement was a logical response to the growth of unemployment and poverty. All local authorities like to be seen to be doing something positive: employing welfare rights staff is a tangible demonstration of concern for people on low incomes and brings extra money into the local economy.

There has always been a problem with benefit take-up rates. In large part this arises from the nature of the means-tested benefits system. Welfare rights advisers thus quickly moved from advising individuals to undertaking publicity campaigns about benefit entitlement. Such techniques were clearly a more useful method of reaching people than any number of individual consultations.

The never-ending round of changes to social security legislation since 1979 has meant that there have been many reductions in benefit entitlement. Often publicity campaigns have been run specifically to encourage people to claim before a negative change takes effect. Welfare rights advisers have pioneered this approach to welfare politics. They have also developed expertise in debt and housing matters because of the links between poverty, debt and homelessness, and this is an interesting extension of their field of influence.

Although the appointment of welfare rights advisers is a comparatively recent development, welfare rights work is not. Advice on benefit matters has been a feature of the work of many people in the welfare state for many years. The relationship between poverty and other social problems, together with the need to inject independence into a benefits system that is frequently badly administered, means that many human service professionals have become involved in this field. Indeed, it is perhaps one of the few things that different professional groups within the welfare state have in common. Social workers, in particular, have been closely associated with helping to resolve benefit problems, because of their own direct involvement in practical service provision for those on low incomes, their residual income maintenance powers for children and families, and the devastating effect that poverty can have on some individuals, to such an extent that they require social work help.

There were also the Claimants' Unions, which have now all but perished. Claimants' Unions never became large organisations but they espoused nonhierarchical methods of organisation and a reliance on democracy. In the type of society in which we live, such avowedly leaderless groups are at a disadvantage. Claimants' Unions combined the roles of giving advice about legal rights to social security and campaigning politically for improvements to the benefits system. They also undertook direct action, such as sit-ins at social security offices. Membership was constitutionally confined to people who were or had recently been benefit claimants. Claimants' Unions published leaflets about benefit rights and undertook tribunal representation for claimants in general, as well as those who were members. Their activities could be described as a combination of legal and self-advocacy.

Unfortunately the Claimants' Unions declined. Their anarchic and parochially focused style of organisation was perhaps their undoing. Sadly, their demise occurred when such organisations were most needed as unemployment started to rise sharply in the early 1980s. Their lack of formal links to anyone – and in particular, the wider labour movement – clearly did not help when trade union members were being made redundant. It is also the case that many activists in the Claimants' Unions progressed into employment in advice work and thus into paid work as welfare rights advisers.

The growth of the welfare rights movement in local authorities – with better resources and more political influence than Claimants' Unions – as well as in formal advice settings meant that the ramshackle web of Claimants' Unions compared poorly in the eyes of service users.

This growth was mirrored by a parallel growth in the voluntary sector – particularly in advice agencies. There was also the development of law centres in the late 1960s and 1970s. Law centres offered skilled legal assistance for those on low incomes, and it was inevitable that their areas of expertise focused on the legal problems of their clients. This, naturally, meant that they developed skills in welfare rights work and used the rules to obtain substantial improvements for those on low incomes who had previously not been able to enforce their rights.

Advocacy in human service professions

There is an encouraging amount of acceptance among those in human ser-vice professions of the role of advocacy. In social work, medicine and nurs-ing there is literature to confirm the acceptance of advocacy as one of the tools for helping people and ensuring that their rights are upheld, even though literature on the skills needed in advocacy is lacking.

To deny advocacy as a legitimate part of the process of helping people sur-vive life's rigours is to deny the reality of life itself. As Davies has succinctly put it in a classic text of social work practice: 'Strategies of change in social work might sometimes need to be directed, not at the client, but at dysfunc-tional elements in the client's environment.'[12] Davies goes on to describe two forms of advocacy in social work: personal advocacy and structural advo-cacy. The former focuses on the individual's need and the latter on a commu-nity or group. 'In either case, the assumption is that the social worker has skills and qualities or access to resources that are likely to tip the balance in the favour of those whose interests would otherwise be overlooked or over-ridden.'[13]

Coulshed, another writer on social work theory, places advocacy among the skills to be used when trying to obtain resources for a client.[14] Advocacy is seen as a practical skill and is divorced from the philosophical basis of advocacy that is, primarily, concerned with depersonalising a problem. Seeing advocacy as just a method of performing mundane practical tasks is to overlook the debilitating potential of other social work methods, with their emphasis on personal failure and personal success amidst worldly cata-strophe.

Coulshed also describes a useful theoretical framework for all advocacy – not just that undertaken by social workers. Advocacy should take place where the professional is in situations where 'having to fight to secure justice or to combat the abuse of power, perhaps by a higher authority, then com-petitive tactics are in order. Where parties are negotiating towards agree-ment rather than to gain advantage, then collaborative elements are to the fore.'[15]

There is also the concept of task-centred casework. An immensely practi-cal method of helping people, task-centred casework is an attempt to place the jumble of undifferentiated structural problems (i.e. the combination of poor health, bad housing and inadequate income that many people grapple with daily) in some form of order, and to impose a therapeutic gloss. It has been found to be an effective form of helping in some situations, and it does require a more egalitarian approach than the psychodynamic models of social work.

A major, though dated, theoretical work on social work, *Theories of Social*

Casework, edited by Roberts and Nee, briefly addresses the role of social worker as advocate:

> questions of environmental effects on personality and environment as a dynamic in change led to the issue of the caseworker as advocate ... [There is] a distinction between 'case advocacy' (caseworker as advocate for the individual and his welfare) and 'policy advocacy' (caseworker as advocate of societal or agency policy change) ... caseworkers have been and continue to be advocates for their individual clients ... it has been an ingredient in treatment throughout the history of casework.[16]

One can excuse the pejorative use of the word 'treatment' in the above quote (it was a fashionable but patronising concept at the time) but it does show, once again, that effective social work practice must include advocacy.

Roberts and Nee's book also has some useful things to say about the dangers of advocacy:

> The use of clients by caseworkers in policy advocacy could develop into conscious as well as unconscious exploitation of clients' misery and helplessness as surely as the goal of adjustment to his [the client's] environment (which was never a theoretical goal of casework) is alleged to have done. This exploitation will develop unless there is careful work with clients as to what they want for themselves and how much they want to and can involve themselves as citizens, not clients in societal and policy change.[17]

This is helpful advice for any advocate.

Despite the apparent acceptance of advocacy as part of the daily work of many people in human service organisations, including those in social work, there is a dearth of writing on advocacy as a skill in its own right and nothing to show people how to advocate for others in practice. There is also no agreement about terminology, and no common understanding of advocacy as a skill in itself in the same way that, for example, counselling is recognised as a skill.

Advocacy can arise in many situations – as described earlier. Poverty heightens stress and reduces people's ability to live fulfilling lives. It is thus inevitable that social workers and other human service professionals have to act as their advocates. In the case of social work, there are also the residual discretionary financial powers exercised by social workers. When the main income maintenance system fails, one can hardly blame the victims for turning to social workers for practical help!

The most common form of advocacy within helping professions is welfare rights advocacy. This emphasis on money reflects the needs of the service users and is clearly a reflection of the growth of poverty in the 1980s. The massive growth of unemployment is at the heart of this growth of poverty as people with previously secure jobs have been drawn into the ranks of the unwaged.

The lack of job opportunities not only creates problems for the formerly waged but for the waged as well: witness the growth of low-paid work in the 1980s and the depressing effect upon skilled wage levels. Similarly, employment and the chance of participation in society with money in one's pocket has been seriously eroded for people with disabilities, for younger pensioners and for single parents. Successive studies have also shown that unemployment contributes directly to chronic ill health and family breakdown. The helping professions would be strangely aloof if they did not respond to this major change in the lives of their service users. Advocacy is one practical method of responding. The influence of the 'softer' forms of advocacy described earlier should also not be overlooked.

Doel and Shardlow see advocacy as part of the role of social workers. They have a very loose definition of advocacy: ' . . . the practitioner's work on behalf of the client . . . the skills of expressing your own view, even when it conflicts with other people's. The expressed views may indeed be on behalf of a client.'[18] My criticism of this approach is that it is not specific enough and it fails to distinguish between advocacy for groups and advocacy for individuals. It also, critically, fails to distinguish between structured problems and unstructured problems, appearing to see negotiation and assertiveness as the only ways of resolving issues and conflicts. However, Doel and Shardlow *do* emphasise that advocacy can concern unstructured problems – such as trying to resist demands that a person should be admitted to a residential home when that person wishes to remain in the community. Such issues are as important to the individual concerned as a dispute about entitlement to a social security benefit.

The distinction between advocacy on what have been described as bounded problems and advocacy on those described as unbounded problems is important. Structured problems have been characterised as bounded problems and unstructured ones as unbounded. Bounded problems are best resolved by a more litigious approach than unbounded problems. People working in human service organisations are often working with individuals on unbounded problems, so it can be easy to fail to recognise when the problem is bounded and thus needs quite different skills to resolve. Bounded problems are characterised by rules, regulations and procedures – they will have a clear structure for resolving disputes or differences of interpretation. These procedures will form the basis for any action. Unbounded problems are based more on inter-personal issues and lack a clearly regulated structure to fall back on. With unbounded problems, it will be necessary to engage the other side in a solution and to work constructively towards it, and the more robust versions of advocacy will not be helpful.

Bounded problems

- Have a limited timescale
- Have clear priorities
- Have limited applications
- Can be treated as a separate matter
- Are discrete
- Usually involve a limited number of people
- You will know what needs to be done
- You will know what the problem is
- You will know what would be a solution

Unbounded problems

- Appear to have no solutions
- Have longer, more uncertain timescales
- The implications are greater but more uncertain
- Are not discrete and can't be disentangled from their context
- Usually involve more people
- You will not know what needs to be known
- You will not be sure what the problem is.[19]

Here are some examples of bounded and unbounded problems:

Bounded problems

- Refusal of a Social Fund grant
- Exclusion of a child from school
- A decision about housing for a homeless person
- The decision to allocate a limited amount of support to a person living in the community
- Debt problems

Unbounded problems

- Many decisions about medical treatment
- Joint planning of a new project with another organisation
- A complaint about a colleague's conduct
- Negotiating a contract with a supplier
- Most inter-personal disputes

Advocacy in nursing and medicine

While much of this chapter has concentrated on the place of advocacy in social work, one must not ignore the role of advocacy in other helping professions. While there may be a different emphasis, there is, none the less, an ethical basis and framework for advocacy by other human service professionals – especially in medicine. Because advocacy is often primarily concerned with obtaining resources for someone and helping them, it sits comfortably with a range of other activities.

The greatest advances in medical care have been when medicine has turned from individualised treatment plans to addressing issues affecting whole groups. For example, the eradication of smallpox, and the nineteenth-century public health movement, can be viewed as medical models of group advocacy. It has long been accepted that medical staff should speak out on social and economic problems that affect people's health.

Any literature search on advocacy in medicine will throw up hundreds of references. Quite different approaches to advocacy have developed in nursing compared to mainstream medicine. Most of the developments in medical advocacy in medicine have taken place in the United States, where the leading role of insurance companies and the tendency to over-treat means that independent medical guardians are important in making sure that patients receive the appropriate treatment at the right price. Such advocacy will often be concerned with unbounded problems, though the intrusion of legal aspects associated with insurance can mean that bounded problems are also involved. Thus, in the USA, one reads comments such as :

> I have frequently felt that physicians are at their professional best in their role as patient advocates. The traditional extent of our advocacy is perhaps broader than we realise . . . our advocacy must increasingly address societal as well as individual issues . . . our advocacy can provide an element of informed and compassionate health care planning and delivery that is available from no other source.[20]

In the UK, the availability of universal free healthcare has meant that advocacy to protect the patient's pocket has not been required in the past. However, practitioners indicate that the growth of private healthcare, phenomena such as fundholding GPs and the creeping selectivity of the National Health Service, are leading to the development of similar advocacy by doctors in the UK. Doctors have also long had to act as advocates for public health reforms, for better housing and employment.

Within nursing, advocacy has a long history. Florence Nightingale's efforts to improve the basic healthcare of wounded soldiers in the Crimean War involved her acting as an advocate against the medical and military establishment of the time. When one turns to the literature one finds corroboration in statements such as:

nurses have long acknowledged an advocacy role on behalf of individuals but clearly this may not be the case at the policy level.[21]

Advocacy is an important part of the role of the registered nurse . . . being prepared to act as an advocate if required is part of the duty of any nurse . . . advocacy aims to facilitate outcomes which the patient would have wished for had he been in a position to make his own decisions.[22]

In a wide-ranging discussion, Cahill examines various definitions of advocacy in nursing. These are very similar to those used earlier in this chapter, but Cahill further states:

in nursing, the parallel definition of advocacy is the act of 'informing the patient of his rights in a particular situation, making sure that he has all the necessary information to make an informed decision, supporting him in the decision he makes, and protecting and safeguarding interests' . . . advocacy can thus be seen as a necessary part of a therapeutic relationship.[23]

The advocacy role of nurses has been formalised by both the International Council of Nurses and the UK's Code of Professional Conduct. Cahill views these as:

clearly expecting practitioners to accept a role as advocate on behalf of their patients, thereby ensuring that they have enough information to exercise control over their own healthcare, their legal and moral rights are respected, and healthcare resources are adequate to provide an appropriate quality and quantity of nursing.

So, apart from lawyers, nurses appear to be the only professional group to have their role as advocates enshrined in rules of professional conduct.

Advocacy in nursing can include ensuring that a vegetarian patient has the right type of food, ensuring that someone who cannot act for themselves is given the right care and treatment and, with the changing role of community nurses (especially involving people with learning disabilities or mental health problems), advocacy increasingly involves advocating against other organisations on housing, employment or financial matters.

A particular area of difficulty for nurses can involve advocating against a doctor on treatment issues – for example, advocating that a patient who has become disturbed should not be medicated. This is an unbounded problem, and one where the nurse will be at a disadvantage against the inherent power of the higher-paid and higher-status doctor; particularly good assertion and negotiation skills will be needed. The Code of Professional Conduct makes allowances for such conflicts and sets out rules on how medical disagreements should be resolved.

Advocacy in nursing is also at a disadvantage in the individualisation of problems: 'it will be important for professional organisations of nurses both in the UK and other countries to speak up on behalf of clients and patients who are unable to identify health problems and solutions for themselves'.[24] It is also apparent that advocacy by nurses is only considered applicable when patients are unable to express their own views. How far this fits with the model of ethics proposed in Chapter 2 is a matter for debate.

A rights perspective

The word 'rights' is frequently used in advocacy. This is perhaps not surprising as they are the fulcrum upon which advocacy balances. One major advantage of advocacy is that it brings a rights-based perspective into individually focused work – work which can otherwise lead to the individual being blamed for the failures of the external world. By bringing in a rights-based perspective in one area of a person's life it is likely that such a perspective will develop in other areas. This means that the helping process becomes more egalitarian and democratic, with the service users in a stronger position because they are influencing the direction of the activity.

Thus it is hardly surprising that advocates often speak of the importance of the concept of 'citizenship'. Citizenship is a value concept that encompasses the range of obligations and rights a society grants its members. There are said to be three basic elements to the idea of citizenship:

- Political
- Social
- Civil

Realising one's rights in any of the above areas is to realise one's rights as a citizen, because non-citizens are denied rights. So, it is essential that, where rights are unclear or the opportunity to enforce them is limited, the question of citizenship is addressed to push back the limitations for those affected.

One can view the political element of citizenship as the right to participate in the exercise of power. At its very least this involves voting, but it should extend to lobbying political decision makers and the right to become a decision maker oneself.

The social element of citizenship involves the right to enjoy minimum standards of welfare and security. Clearly the right and ability to have access to adequate education and social security are fundamental. The lack of such rights or, more commonly, the clouding of those rights in obscure language and procedures means that many people are effectively denied the chance to be full citizens of the society in which they live.

Finally, the civil element of citizenship was defined by Marshall as 'liberty

of the person, freedom of speech, thought and faith, the right to own property and to conclude valid contracts and the right to justice'.[25] Marshall discussed the importance of access to appropriate institutions in order to
remedy breaches of the rights of citizenship.

The importance of the concept of citizenship is that it clarifies the basis of
advocacy and it reflects the philosophical basis of much activity in the welfare state. Human service professionals are primarily concerned with the
needs of an individual. To satisfy those needs in an unequal society, service
users must turn needs into rights. If those rights mean anything they must be
capable of enforcement, and thus the intervention of a third party – the advocate – will often be needed. Advocacy has also been given a degree of
respectability by recent developments in new models of welfare provision. A
new emphasis on the rights of service users as consumers of welfare services
formalises the moral rights to receive a service, as from the political right
have come market-based philosophies about the welfare state. These have
seen participation by consumers as essential to ensure that consumers have
choice. However, they should be treated with caution:

> Welfare users are not equivalent to consumers in the world of commerce. They
> include some of the most powerless and stigmatized members of society. For
> some, ill-health, frailty or disability may further hamper their ability to 'shop
> around' and make untrammelled choices in a marketplace of care services.
> Consumers of . . . services are rarely in a position to 'take their custom else-
> where'.[26]

At the same time various writers have emphasised that consumer participation is not only more efficient because it ensures a better match between
provision and need, but it is also essential to preserve people's rights and
dignity. Thus rights to a service mean that the consumer has a right to accept
or decline a standard of service, and formal rights must follow if those rights
are to be capable of enforcement. However, formal rights on their own are
not enough. There has to be information and clear, legally enforceable rights
to services if clients and advocates are to be effective in their participation in
decision making and obtaining services. There must also be a reduction in
the 'professional' barriers around service provision so that clients are treated
in a more egalitarian manner. Advocates have a key role in achieving this, as
the vast majority of people make poor self-advocates – especially when, of
necessity, it involves parading one's own needs and failures before welfare
professionals who have greater power and status.

At the same time that consumerist and rights-based views of welfare provision have developed, there have been major changes in social conditions.
The growth of poverty, low wages and homelessness have a major impact
upon the users of all welfare services. Research shows clear links between
poverty and ill health, and that the differences in health between rich and

poor have grown considerably during the 1980s and early 1990s.[27] Other statistics point to links between poverty and demands for personal and housing services.

The gap between rich and poor has grown and is witnessed by the increase in the numbers on means-tested benefits, the growth of low-paid, insecure work, and the rise in personal indebtedness. At the same time, official unemployment has remained near 3 million – a figure previously regarded as politically suicidal – as the economy has been restructured away from traditional industries to service and secondary industries that require a highly skilled core workforce and a large, low-paid, low-skilled, flexible pool of labour for peripheral tasks.

The growth of poverty has created pressure on welfare budgets and led to countless restrictions. Advocacy has developed as one response to such developments, and has been seen as useful in highlighting injustices on both an individual and a collective level when it successfully challenges accepted legal interpretations or organisational practices. This applies particularly to advocacy on housing and social security issues.

Whatever the context of advocacy, it needs a firm ethical basis if it is to be effective. It therefore follows that clients must have access to advocates to make advocacy effective and to redress the imbalance in power between the providers of services and the consumer. It is perhaps ironic that right-wing welfare philosophy has meant that advocacy can be seen as a perfectly proper method of making consumer demands. However, it remains to be seen whether or not the establishment can tolerate really effective advocacy on anything other than a small scale. There are already many instances of welfare organisations withdrawing financial or political support from vigorous local advocates.

The concepts of rights to services, rights to an adequate income and decent housing, rights to humane treatment by welfare organisations and the right to participate in society on equal terms are at the heart of advocacy. They drive the advocate's actions. This naturally leads us to consider the ethical principles behind advocacy in Chapter 2.

References

1   Harvey QC, C. P. (1958), *The Advocate's Devil*, cited in Pannick, D. (1993), *Advocates*, Oxford University Press.
2   See *The MIND Guide to Advocacy – Empowerment in Action* (1992), London: MIND Publications.
3   Report on Social Insurance and Allied Services (1942), Cmnd 6406 (known as the Beveridge Report).

4   See Small, E. (1991), 'People, Print and Power', *Social Work Today*, 7 March.
5   Lindow, V. (1992), 'Just Lip-service', *Nursing Times*, 2 December, **88**, (49), 63.
6   Sang, R. and O'Brien, J. (1984), *Advocacy*, King Edward's Hospital Fund for London.
7   Butler, K. and Forrest, A. (1991), in Winn, E. (ed.), *Power to the People – The key to responsive services in health and social care*, London: Kings Fund Centre.
8   Simons, K. (1994), 'Cloudy Outlook', *Community Care*, 3 February.
9   Ibid.
10 Philpot, T. (1993), 'Lip Service that gags advocacy', *The Guardian*, 17 March.
11 Pannick, D. (1993), *Advocates*, Oxford University Press.
12 Davies, M. (1994), *The Essential Social Worker* (3rd edn), Aldershot: Arena.
13 Ibid.
14 Coulshed, V. (1991), *Social Work Practice – An Introduction* (2nd edn), Macmillan.
15 Ibid.
16 Simon, B. (1970), in Roberts, R. and Nee, R. (eds), *Theories of Social Casework*, University of Chicago Press.
17 Ibid.
18 Doel, M. and Shardlow, S. (1993), *Social Work Practice*, Aldershot: Gower.
19 Watson, L. and Watson, N. (1986), *Planning and Managing Change*, Milton Keynes: Open University.
20 Klocke, F. (1988), 'Physicians as Advocates in the 1980s and 1990s', *Journal of the American College of Cardiology*, July, **12**, (1), 286–7.
21 Clarke, M. (1989), Patient/Client Advocates', *Journal of Advanced Nursing*, **14**, 513–14.
22 Carpenter, D. (1988), 'Advocacy', *Nursing Times*, Open Learning Programme Module P9, 24 June and 1 July, **88**, (26) and (27).
23 Cahill, J. (1994), 'Are You Prepared to be their Advocate?', *Professional Nurse*, **9**, (6), 371–5.
24 Clarke, op. cit.
25 Marshall, T. H. (1975), *Social Policy*, Hutchinson Educational.
26 Biehal, N. (1993), 'Changing Practice: Participation, Rights and Community Care', *British Journal of Social Work*, **23**, 443–58.
27 For example, see Phillimore, P., Beatie, A. and Townsend, P. (1994), 'Widening Inequality of Health in Northern England, 1981–91', *British Medical Journal*, **308**: 1125–8; and Whitehead, M. (1987), *The Health Divide*, London: Health Education Council.

2 Principles

More definitions

This chapter covers the ethical aspects of advocacy. Ethics – the science of morals, the philosophy of behaviour and conduct – is important to advocates because it sets down the ground rules for operation, and provides a clear focus so that their efforts are concentrated on the task in hand and not distracted when a tangential, ethical problem arises. By having a sound ethical base, ethical dilemmas are minimised.

Many professions already have well-developed formal ethical codes. Others may mimic the established codes or operate with informal, unwritten codes based on a common understanding. Welfare professionals employed by organisations may find that ethical rules are formalised by incorporation into contracts of employment or other conditions of service.

Whichever setting we work in we all use jargon, so it will be useful to clarify some of the jargon used by advocates before discussing the ethical ground rules.

Client

This replaces the vague and misleading term 'customer'. Customers have spending power, but such a prerogative is not available to most users of the welfare state, and many argue it would distort the equitable supply of services if it were. Similarly, 'service user' implies helplessness even if it is preferable to the term 'customer'.

The term 'patients' is frequently applied inaccurately, and such people are usually not the caricatures of chronic indecision that it suggests. It also implies that they are ill when their state of health may be similar to many others who are not so labelled.

The use of the term 'client' seems to have drifted out of fashion in social work. It was never fashionable in other circles, perhaps because it implied that the recipient was valued or had an opinion to be listened to, whereas welfare organisations sometimes wanted to impose actions on that person, and not be distracted by tiresome statements concerning what it felt like to be a recipient. The use of the term 'partner' is a laudable attempt at ensuring equity in the advocacy relationship; however, it does not adequately describe the relationship in advocacy work unconnected with Citizen Advocacy. The term 'client' does not have the dishonest, bureaucratic connotations of other expressions, and it does serve to describe the instructional relationship between advocate and service user.

It is unfortunate that the expression 'client' has taken on a pejorative meaning and can be used in a patronising manner. This may arise as much from the lack of power of users of the human services as anything inherent in the term itself. Describing a client as a service user or a customer does not give them any more power if their objective situation is unchanged.

A helpful dictionary definition of 'client' is 'one who is served'. It is precisely the notion of service to the client that underpins the ethical basis of advocacy. Another definition, though one that is less common, is 'one who has an advocate'. Consequently the term 'client' will be used throughout the rest of this book to describe the partner, customer, service user, recipient, etc., of advocacy services.

The other side

This is lawyers' jargon for the other party involved in the advocacy; 'opponents' is another common expression. Neither term is necessarily pejorative, and they do make it clear whose side the advocate is on. Advocacy is not a partnership between advocate and opponent because the nature of the problems dealt with makes such a relationship both unworkable and unhelpful. Thus the terms 'other side' and 'opponent' encapsulate the concept of service to the client: they show where the advocate's primary obligations lie.

Principled Advocacy

Principled Advocacy is an approach to advocacy in human service settings which lays down a structure for advocates to follow and clarifies their ethical obligations. Principled Advocacy is a new approach, and I do not claim that it has all the answers for every situation or problem. But it is helpful because it establishes the boundaries of activity for advocates and provides a ready-made formula so that advocates minimise ethical dilemmas.

Principled Advocacy is based on the professional conduct rules for solicitors, many of which also apply to barristers. The principles should apply throughout the advocate's actions on behalf of a client.

All the principles are related to each other and none can be viewed in total isolation, though each covers a distinct ethical issue.

Principle 1

'Act in the client's best interests'

Ethical puzzle no. 1

Consider the ethical dilemmas displayed in the following case-study. It raises a number of practice issues that may be found in various professional settings and also shows the link with various advocacy skills.

A social worker receives a telephone call from a benefit fraud investigator. The social worker is involved in helping a father looking after two small children who were removed from the care of their mother (the father's ex-partner) following abuse. The mother has continued to claim benefit for the children. The fraud investigator insists that the social worker provide the dates when the children stayed with the father.

Issues

1 Confidentiality.
2 Action against the mother for benefit fraud might result in her being resentful towards her ex-husband and the social worker. This could affect her relationship with the children.
3 It might be in the children's best interests for their mother to be out of circulation for a few months, or for her to have a criminal conviction to undermine any future claim for custody by her.
4 Action for benefit fraud may well mean she has to repay the money. Her standard of living will be reduced as money is paid back. Is this helpful?
5 Is it really a fraud officer on the phone? It might be a private investigator or a nosy neighbour.
6 Whoever is on the phone, shouldn't this sort of request be put in writing, citing the precise legal authority?
7 Benefit fraud by individuals is an understandable response by people trying to live on benefits that are, by all objective measures, inadequate.
8 Through receiving more money than her entitlement the mother has been able to buy the children birthday presents.
9 Even if she did receive more money than she was entitled to, the benefit rules are indecipherable and confusing. Who says it's fraud? It may be a wholly innocent mistake.

It is perhaps self-evident that the advocate should always act in the client's best interests, but it is worth restating. It is a principle which is easily overlooked when acting as an advocate because of the many pressures to compromise the vigour of one's advocacy or to work in partnership with the other side.

Principle 1 means that advocates should constantly remember who they are acting for and what is the ultimate purpose of those actions. Acting in the client's interests may also mean that the advocate has to steer the client away from a particular course of action that the client would like to pursue – for example, where the suggested course of action is likely to have a detrimental physical, material or psychological effect, or where the same result could be achieved through another course of action.

Acting in the client's best interests can also create a dilemma. What if the client's best interests are not in the best interests of society or a wider group of clients? For example, the client who wants to pursue an appeal which could result in accepted legal interpretation being altered to the detriment of others, or the abusing parent who wishes to regain custody of their child. There is no easy solution to such a dilemma. Ultimately it will depend on the advocate's own values and judgement, but the dilemma can be minimised by applying Principle 2.

Acting in the best interests of a client can also, occasionally, involve the farcical, as the following example shows:

> Advocacy may require a professional devotion to causes hopeless beyond redemption even by the most skilful of exponents of the craft. In 1616 a defendant pleaded infancy as a defence to an action. However, it was found by sufficient proof, by oath and by examination of the church book, that he was of the age of 63 years.[1]

Principle 2

'Act in accordance with the client's wishes and instructions'

Ethical puzzle no. 2

Good interviewing and listening skills are necessary to obtain instructions, and it is important neither to jump to conclusions nor to prejudge a situation.

A worker in an advice centre sees a male client in his twenties. He says that he would like help finding somewhere else to live, as the bedsit where he lives is damp and gloomy. He also says that his landlord is intimidating and he would not like to upset him. The advice worker quickly comes to the conclusion that the client has no prospect of obtaining housing in the public sector and asks the client to leave matters with him. The advice worker then drafts a letter to the landlord claiming compensation for damp as it is a breach of the landlord's obligations to his tenant. A week later the client comes back saying that the landlord has said he wants him to leave as he is a trouble-maker.

Issues

1 What exactly did the client wish? Was it:

   - Compensation?
   - A fight with his landlord?
   - Somewhere else to live?
   - A council property?
   - His landlord to treat him better?
   - A friendly chat with the advice worker?

2 Would the client's wishes have been altered by giving him advice about his rights?
3 Has the advice worker been too hasty in reaching a conclusion? Should the matter have been researched a bit more? For example, if there had been more questioning and listening could it have led the advice worker to conclude that the client did, after all, have a right to council housing under the homelessness legislation?
4 Should the advice worker take other action against the landlord, for example by reporting him to the local authority harassment officer, or telling other tenants about the landlord's behaviour?

There is an instructional relationship between advocates and clients which is fundamental. This is most marked in any form of legal advocacy but also characterises Citizen Advocacy. The advocate's actions have to be driven by the client's wishes and instructions if the client is to have any sense of ownership of the problem and its resolution. Developing the instructional relationship is thus one way in which the advocate can develop a healthy helping relationship with the client. It adds balance to the inherent power differences in most helping relationships, where the helper will have greater professional, economic or psychological power than the client.

This can fundamentally alter the dynamics where the helper is used to a more compliant relationship, as the client is now in the driving seat rather than being driven along by the professional desires of the helper. It is important to recognise this and to recognise that these altered dynamics can be uncomfortable for some in helping professions. It can also be a challenge for clients who may be unused to exercising this sort of power.

No advocacy will be effective unless the client is committed to it. Many clients will not find it easy to develop any sense of ownership of the solution – an attitude perhaps formed after years of powerlessness and repeated refusals from the other side. A lack of commitment by the client will hamper the efforts of the best advocate. It can also lead to the advocate acting in complete isolation and being unable to respond to attacks from the other side.

Equally, the instructional relationship enables the advocate to identify the facts, the options and remedies, and to know when the expertise of a third party is required. Sometimes it may be necessary to lead the client in order to obtain instructions – the client might benefit from considered and honest advice about their situation or from gradual confidence-building. Taking instructions will also involve the advocate in listening to the client. It is easy to push the client when the advocate is fired with enthusiasm for the client's cause. Using listening skills will enable the client to have more control over the advocate and the advocate to give better advice. There is a clear link between the process of obtaining instructions and the stages of advocacy discussed in Chapter 11.

The advocate's duty is to safeguard the interests of the client fearlessly – even in the face of considerable hostility. This duty may involve ignoring any consequences for the advocate. Such a duty cannot exist unless it is in the context of acting in the client's best interests; sometimes clients will want to instruct the advocate in an inappropriate way – for example, they may wish the advocate to undertake something illegal or dangerous. Clearly the advocate has the option to refuse to accept such instructions. This is honest and straightforward. The clients will know where they stand.

In other cases, the instructions will be counter to the ethics or morality of the advocate. Advocates need to reconcile their own ethics with their duty to do the best for the client. If reconciliation cannot be achieved, the advocate should decline instructions. If it happens more than occasionally, the advocate needs to consider whether they are really able to advocate at all. Usually the conflict between one's own values and the instructions from the client will be overridden by the pressures of the implicit expectation of the employer that the advocate is in the business of helping clients. The debate about conflicts is best kept informal, rather than being imposed upon the work with clients.

Finally, the essence of acting on instructions is to avoid the problems described in the second ethical puzzle. It should all start and end with 'This is what I *think* we can do. What do you *want* me to do?'

Principle 3

'Keep the client properly informed'

Ethical puzzle no. 3

Proper instructions can't be obtained unless the client is fully informed. It is also a hallmark of courtesy and good practice.

A housing officer is helping a young single parent to obtain a Social Fund grant

---

from the Department of Social Security so that she can set up home. She needs a cooker, curtains, carpets and a variety of basic household items. She has two young children under 5 and she has a social worker. The social worker is involved because there are concerns about the children's development, the poor relationship between mother and children, and the repeated instances of minor injuries from over-chastisement.

The housing officer is contacted over the phone by the Department of Social Security, who ask if there is any risk of the children going into care. They say that they need this information to assess whether she qualifies for a Social Fund grant since it will reduce the likelihood of a member of the family entering institutional care.

The housing officer, eager to help, says that it is possible that the children could go into care. The grant is still refused on the grounds that the client's needs are too low a priority for the amount of money available in the budget.

The client asks for a review and reads in the casepapers sent out for the review that her children might be taken into care. She goes into the housing office and tells the housing officer that he is '. . . full of shit and don't you ever come near my house again or you'll be sorry. And that's a promise not a threat.' The housing officer phones the police to report this, and his manager instructs all the staff in the office that 'this woman must not be seen on her own'.

Issues

1 Why was the phone used? The matter was urgent and it can be quicker to give information by phone, but it can lead to misunderstandings and errors of judgement because of the lack of time for a considered response.
2 Why didn't the officer ask the client for instructions on this matter?
3 Did the officer have authority from the client or her social worker to disclose information? What instructions had been obtained from the client about this?
4 Why didn't the officer explore other arguments for obtaining a Social Fund grant?
5 Why did the officer apparently just accept the question posed by the Department of Social Security (the other side)? What independent research was undertaken?
6 Given the client's reaction and the subsequent response from the housing organisation, does it not indicate a lack of recognition that the client has rights and that the role of advocate cannot be separated from the rest of the work being undertaken? The lack of consultation with the client and the lack of information given to her effectively destroyed this advocate's relationship with the client.

It is clearly impractical to inform the client about everything that is going on. At best it will make the advocacy slow and laborious. At worst, it paralyses it. But it is important, both from an ethical and a practical point of view, to make sure that clients are aware of what is being said and done on their behalf.

Sometimes it may be difficult to distil the complexities of advocacy into everyday language. It may be even more difficult to explain the apparently bizarre logic of one's actions. However, it is important to remember that keeping the client informed is so much easier if the advocate is in the habit of doing so.

From an ethical viewpoint, it is important to keep the client informed as it ensures that the client is aware of the advocate's work for them. This complements the principle of the client instructing the advocate: information is power, and involving the client is easier if the information and power is shared. Obviously, it also provides for accountability, which is especially important for advocates who provide their services without charge. If the advocate does charge, this entails accountability. People will be reluctant to part with their money unless they can see some worthwhile result, and that an acceptable service has been provided.

However, this is not an argument for introducing charges for advice-giving by welfare professionals. Levying a charge will not, by itself, guarantee accountability: witness the millions of dissatisfied customers of the private sector – travel agents who book the wrong holiday, solicitors who over-charge, builders who do shoddy work, garages that misrepair cars, estate agents who do nothing, shops that sell defective goods and refuse refunds. There are also many people who are persuaded to pay a charge and who are unaware of or unable to enforce their rights not to pay. Even if a charge were to be made for advice and advocacy, the ethical principle of keeping the client properly informed would still be necessary to minimise the problems associated with charging in other domains.

There are also practical reasons for keeping the client properly informed. The advocate may have misunderstood the client's wishes and instructions: updating the client can provide an opportunity to clarify these. It also gives an opportunity for the client to change their instructions. Similarly, it can help the advocate obtain more information from a client, and it helps put clients on an equal footing with the other side because they know what is happening; it also helps to reinforce the concept that the advocate is acting on the client's behalf.

The other side may not be aware that the advocate is acting in an ethical manner for the client. It can be particularly useful to record the other side's comments about the client and to copy those letters that contain negative remarks. The other side should not be allowed to make judgements about people's rights on the basis of their prejudices regarding the deservedness of the client. Copying their correspondence to the client is likely to reduce the chances of them doing this, and also makes it easier to challenge such assumptions.

So, how should the advocate keep the client properly informed? There are many easy steps that can be taken, and readers will have their own ideas. Some might include:

- Sending copies of all the advocate's correspondence on the matter to the client
- Drafting correspondence so that, when it concerns the client personally, it is written in the client's name and then passed to them for approval and signature
- Making phone calls to the other side when the client is present

Had such practices taken place in the third ethical puzzle, it is almost certain that the client would not have been discriminated against in such a way, and the aggressive conclusion would have been avoided.

Principle 4

'Carry out instructions with diligence and competence'

Ethical puzzle no. 4

If you offer to do something, make sure that you do it. Also, know the limits of your expertise.

A man aged 87 has a visit from a local pressure group for older people. The visit has been prompted by a call from his doctor, who is concerned that he may be in need of various support services. The visitor is keen on the idea of advocacy.

The client is happy to receive a visit, and they start to discuss various issues about the care and support he gets. Among the many matters they talk about is the client's need for a phone. He has done without one all his life, but would like to be able to contact his daughter who lives some distance away. As his health is now increasingly precarious, he would like the security of a phone to be able to ring the doctor. It would also be useful for his home help, who sometimes has changes in her rota. She would then be able to contact him and let him know when she would be with him.

However, there is just no way that he can afford a phone, and he asks the visitor if he knows how he can get the installation cost paid. The client is happy to pay the rental, he just can't find the lump sum for a connection charge. The visitor promises to investigate the matter and get back to the client.

The visitor goes back to his office. He rings the local social work office and asks if they are able to help with the cost of a phone. The pressure group has a very good working relationship with the social work team, and they are on first-name terms with all the staff. They operate on a quid pro quo basis. The duty social worker to whom he speaks says that it is nearing the end of the financial year and that it is very unlikely that they can help as there is almost nothing left in the phone

---

there are insufficient funds available to pay for a phone, but suggesting that if an application were made in April the situation might be more optimistic. The visitor calls on the client when he is next in the area (about a month later) and gives him a copy of the letter. They decide to pursue the possibility of obtaining finance from a local charity, but the client is reluctant to follow this course of action as he feels it is too much trouble.

Issues

1   The advocate appears to have acted promptly, to have involved the client in some of the process and to have acted on the wishes of the client, i.e. the client wanted a phone installed so the advocate has tried to obtain one.
2   What evidence is there that the advocate has researched the problem?
3   Was the promptness of the advocate's actions affected at all by their good working relationship with the local social work team? Would the advocate have been so keen if the local team was unfriendly and unhelpful?
4   Has the advocate been:

- Diligent ?
- Competent?

The two are different.
5   Should the advocate have made sure that the general shortage of funds was raised as an issue with the senior managers of the organisation?
6   We can only assume that:

- The advocate had fully dealt with all the other relevant areas, such as the possibility of maximising income through the benefits system.
- The social work office had undertaken a formal community care assessment. If they hadn't they should have. If they had, there are many rights issues which follow from the assessment.
7   Is the time delay of a month in giving a response to the client acceptable?

It is not in anyone's interests if instructions are not acted upon with the thoroughness and competence that is required. The key words are 'diligence' and 'competence'. Advocates are not expected to be perfect, nor to never make mistakes. Advocates thus need to recognise when outside help is required, and to know the limits of their expertise. This could, of course, be the ultimate opt-out clause for the reluctant advocate who would rather someone else undertook the advocacy.

Many people working in human service organisations have access to considerable quantities of information about their clients. Diligence in advocacy is often a matter of linking the relevant facts in that information to the best interpretation of law or policy. It is thus not too dramatic a shift for welfare professionals to move into advocacy mode. It also shows that, even if the advocacy is passed over to someone else, it is important for the original advocate to remain involved because of the information they hold; for one thing, it saves duplication of effort.

Of course, everyone needs to know their limits. It is unrealistic to expect most people working in human service organisations to develop into advocates competent in all areas. But it is my firm conviction, based on many years' experience, that most people are able to become skilled advocates provided that training and support is available to them. The argument that someone else should deal with the problem is over-simplistic and unrealistic. In many areas there are simply no other agencies skilled or able to assist, and many legal advocates either lack skill or, for various reasons, are not interested in the mixture of social and legal problems that characterise the needs of consumers of welfare services. It is often a case of 'the buck stops here', and this should be recognised when resources are allocated.

One of the most effective methods of developing advocacy among a wider constituency is to develop systems so that people engaging in advocacy have access to good back-up advice services. In my own experience, by ensuring that such an approach is adopted, many less skilled people have been able to become effective advocates for their clients.

Acting diligently and competently also involves effective self-management skills. The advocate needs to respond speedily and efficiently to problems. A particular weakness displayed by some advocates is procrastination. Being stumped by a problem can lead to the advocate not acting at all and putting the matter on one side. This is poor self-management and is not confined to advocacy.

The skills associated with time management are especially pertinent to advocates. Chapter 8 discusses the skills of time management, and there are training courses available on this subject, as well as textbooks on how to organise oneself more effectively. Such skills are by no means only useful in advocacy, and are relevant to almost any activity. Lack of effective self-management can lead to serious mishaps and additional stress for the advocate.

There are also performance targets. All organisations should have basic targets on how speedily customers should be dealt with. It is a basic requirement for ensuring quality and sensitivity to people's needs. It also impresses on managers and other staff the importance of serving the public and not keeping them waiting at the professional's convenience. Diligence can be usefully quantified in various ways and built in as part of performance targets for organisations that engage in advocacy.

Competence involves advocates remembering that they are acting for the client. Consequently, it is not desirable for advocates to rely on the other side for their technical information. They must develop independent, rights-based methods for obtaining the advice and support that is needed.

Finally, the idea that advocates should act diligently and competently links directly to Principle 1: it cannot be in the client's interests if the advocate does not deal with the problem diligently and competently.

Principle 5

'Act impartially and offer frank, independent advice'

Ethical puzzle no. 5

The advocate's primary duty is to the client. This also means being able to say uncomfortable things and not being beholden to the other side.

A community nurse visits one of his patients. The patient is a disabled woman in her fifties who has a degenerative condition. Recently she has started to experience some incontinence. The client asks if she can be provided with incontinence pads. The nurse replies that there is a waiting list as funds are not sufficient to purchase supplies for all those who need them. He promises to discuss the matter with his managers to see if additional funds can be found. After discussion he writes to the client advising that she will have to go on the waiting list, but that he doesn't think that this will be for more than a few weeks.

Issues

1   What evidence is there of the advocate obtaining independent advice on this problem?
2   Some basic research on the legal issues involved would have shown the dubious legality of the health service's practice of running a waiting list for incontinence pads. It is also obviously farcical to have a waiting list for such basic necessities.
3   Has the advocate been compromised by the fact that he is employed by the organisation which is at fault?
4   Why didn't the advocate refer to an independent source of help? Was this possibility discussed? Was there a competent organisation or individual able and willing to offer independent, rights-based advice on this issue?
5   Could the advocate have given some written information to the client about her rights?
6   What are the ethics of involving a carer in a dispute of this nature?

Rights are the essence of effective advocacy. There will be times when a rights-based approach to a problem will be undermined by organisational or personal pressure. This pressure is more likely when the advocate is employed or funded by the organisation which is the other side. It can also occur when the advocate puts a high premium on the importance of friendly working relationships with the other side.

Advocacy is appropriate for resolving structured, bounded problems. In such cases, the most effective approach is to have a firm, businesslike attitude to the other side. A co-operative relationship based on partnership with the other side is not only inappropriate for resolving such problems but would easily lead to a breach of one or other of the tenets of Principled Advocacy. Different approaches are required for different types of problem.

There are a number of key themes:

- Independence of action
- Ignoring one's own prejudices: 'Love the sinner not the sin'
- Conflicts of interest

No one can be an effective advocate if they have to act with one hand tied behind their back. The other side is unlikely to be in such a position, and it does a grave disservice to the client. The binding around the advocate's hands can be internal or external.

Internal conflicts can arise when the advocate feels a crisis of conscience in relation to a client or a situation, or where the issue creates a moral dilemma for the advocate.

External factors which limit the advocate's actions and so prevent the advocate offering frank, independent advice can be matters such as the conflict of interest which can arise when the advocate is employed or funded by the other side. This is perhaps the most common external conflict.

Such a conflict will inevitably arise; but it need not be negative *per se*, so it is important to establish an agreed policy on the handling of conflicts of interest. The policy needs to be flexible and to recognise that advocacy can be positive for everyone. Effective advocacy will, for example, highlight problems in the way that services are provided, and sensible senior managers will view this as positive, rather than the all-too-common insecure response that there is not a problem and the advocate is being unreasonable.

It *is* possible for employees of an organisation to act as advocates against their employer. In fact it is more common than is usually realised. Most of the improvements in the welfare state have come about not because of popular pressure but because of representations made by people who work in the welfare state and who see the gaps in the system in their daily work. The conflict can have serious consequences if the advocate finds that the internal representations they make are ineffective. The choice is then whether to pursue the matter through formal appeals mechanisms and perhaps to litigate. Most organisations would view this as disloyal and would not welcome such actions.

There is also an inbuilt psychological restraint which means that if the advocate does actively assist the client through more litigious means, they may not pursue the matter with the diligence they would otherwise employ when carrying out instructions. However, there are many examples of in-house advocates successfully negotiating a position which does enable them to act as advocates against their own employer. There are also many mature organisations which accept that bodies such as advice centres which they fund have a legitimate and positive role to play by actively challenging and litigating against them. Such actions are indicative of a healthy pluralism that gives voice to the needs of dissatisfied customers. For example, many local authority welfare rights officers undertake advocacy against their own employing body; some councils employ housing advisers and children's rights officers who perform a similar function.

Therefore there is not an absolute ethical bar on advocacy against the provider of funds. It depends on the wisdom, forbearance and maturity of the other side. But it is a sad fact that many such organisations are insecure. They fear advocacy and wish to portray their services as better than they really are by denying that advocacy is anything other than vindictiveness and subversion. Hence one finds that law centres, for example, have not infrequently had their funding withdrawn following a successful piece of lit-igation against their funding local authority.

Of primary importance in avoiding conflicts of interest, as well as comply-ing with the principle that one should act in the client's best interests, is the concept of obtaining independent advice for the advocate. It is often disas-trous to use the other side for advice or help. This is self-evident ethically, but it is surprising how often advocates do so.

At best, the advice given by the other side is unlikely to set out all the rights-based options for a client. At worst the advice will be wrong or mis-leading. Many local authorities thus stress the importance of their staff obtaining advice from an independent perspective, rather than expecting their staff to merely repeat the advice given by the organisation which has caused the problem in the first place. This is very much the approach of local authority welfare rights services, for example.

If the conflict of interest means that the advocate cannot represent the client effectively, then the advocate should refer the client to another advo-cate outside the organisation. There is nothing wrong in doing so, and it might be negligent to do otherwise. Such referral does not mean that you abandon the problem to another person. It is effective practice, as well as good manners, to ensure that the referral takes place in an organised man-ner, with advocates passing over such information and understanding of the legal issues involved as they have.

The conflict which can arise when either the client or the issue is in conflict with one's own values has been considered on p. 30. Needless to say, it will savagely undermine your effectiveness as an advocate if you allow your own views to tempt you away from doing your best for the client. If you find yourself in such a situation, refer the client to someone else and contemplate why you have failed them. Similar considerations apply if there is a financial conflict of interest.

It is also important to refer a client to a competent alternative source of help if there is an overwhelming organisational conflict of interest. Sadly, some organisations view it as a sign of chronic disloyalty if their staff merely suggest that the client obtain independent advice on how to challenge the organisation. It may be worth pointing out that the ombudsman services have criticised organisations that have tried to prevent their staff from doing this, or for failing to inform clients that they should do so.

Principle 5 also refers to the importance of offering frank, independent advice. Sometimes the advocate will have to give bad news to a client. At other times, the options and prospects for resolving a problem may be uncertain, or the other side may be able to make difficulties. People have a right to know where they stand and to be able to make a considered choice based on honest, impartial advice. Thus, being frank is a corollary to independent advice. It also requires the advocate to offer advice dispassionately. A high level of rights-based objectivity is essential.

Principle 6

'The advocate should maintain rules of confidentiality'

The inevitable sanctity of the relationship between advocate and client – a prerequisite to avoiding conflicts of interest – means that advocacy necessarily involves confidentiality.

Clients must feel safe in the knowledge that what they say is confidential. Confidentiality is essential to developing the honest, impartial relationship that must exist between advocate and client. It is also a hallmark of the advocate's independence.

Confidentiality is a much-vaunted ethic, and is perhaps the most common ethical theme for advocates and, indeed, welfare professionals in general. Despite the general acceptance that information given by clients is confidential, there is no general code of confidentiality in many organisations. The obvious exceptions are the legal and medical professions and the Citizens' Advice Bureaux (CAB).

Confidentiality can pose problems. It may need considerable assertiveness to uphold, and conflicts can arise about confidentiality itself. Suppose the client tells you that they have killed someone? There may also be situations where it is in the client's best interests for the advocate to breach confidentiality so as to obtain a result for the client.

Also, confidentiality may not be understood by people within the organisation, as well as those outside. One solution is to have a published code of practice on confidentiality. It is surprising how few of these exist.

The box below outlines the basic policy on confidentiality published by the National Association of Citizens' Advice Bureaux (they also have others which give more detailed guidance). Not only does it provide a useful framework for anyone involved in advice-giving, but it incorporates guidance on how to integrate advocacy on individual cases while also generating publicity about the injustices which may occur in those individual cases so as to influence policy makers.

Confidentiality: Basic principles of the CAB[2]

Basic principle: Citizens' Advice Bureaux offer confidentiality to enquirers. Nothing learned by a bureau from enquirers, including the fact of their visits, will be passed on to anyone outside the Service without their express permission.

1   Since an enquirer's approach for assistance is to the bureau rather than to an individual worker, discussion of cases with either colleagues or specialist advisers within bureaux or with staff of the National Association does not constitute passing on details to a third party.
2   Records of interviews with enquirers should be kept in a safe place. More detailed guidance on the confidentiality of records is available.
3   If the enquirer wishes, a bureau should, however, use these records as far as possible to support the enquirer in any legal proceedings.
4   If, on rare occasions, a bureau is under pressure to breach confidentiality, for whatever reason, the organiser should obtain the agreement and support of either the Area Officer or Central Office on the appropriate course of action.
   4.1   The bureau may be approached by the police for information about an enquirer if they suspect a criminal offence. The bureau should explain the principle of confidentiality and point out that no information about the enquirer, including the fact of any visit s/he has made, can be divulged without the enquirer's express permission. If the member of staff is then subpoenaed [in Scotland, 'cited' in court], whether in a criminal or a civil case, s/he can be compelled to give evidence in court.
   4.2   There may be occasions when a bureau worker either suspects or is certain that a client is involved in or is about to be involved in a criminal activity. No criminal offence is committed by someone who fails to pass on knowledge of a crime, unless either they do so for a reward of some kind or the crime could be construed as a Act of Terrorism.
   4.3   With these exceptions, the principle of confidentiality must always be observed. In cases where bureaux feel that confidentiality must be broken, the procedure laid down in the current circular on practical aspects of confidentiality must be followed.
5   Members of a bureau's Management Committee should not be given any confidential information about enquirers without the enquirers' agreement.
6   In no circumstances should details which could enable an enquirer to be identified, or appear to have been identified, be made public.
   6.1   Bureaux should, however, be willing to make public numbers of callers of a particular type and with composite or fabricated case histories, which must always be described as such.
7   It is a function of the Service to draw attention to areas where law and practice warrant review. In no circumstances, however, must this involve a breach of confidentiality.
8   When participating in preventive work involving the collection of evidence a bureau must continue to observe strictly the confidential nature of its enquirers' problems, unless of course the enquirers have agreed that their experience should be used in order to benefit others.

Conclusion

The six principles behind Principled Advocacy provide an ethical frame-work for all advocacy practice. Without a solid ethical basis, advocacy can become lost, and serious damage may be caused to the client's interests by advocacy that is not rooted in a clear statement of ethics. The six principles form the basis of an ethical code of practice that can be adopted by anyone working in the welfare state who engages in advocacy on behalf of others.

A code of ethics for advocates

1 Act in the client's best interests.
2 Act in accordance with the client's wishes and instructions.
3 Keep the client properly informed.
4 Carry out instructions with diligence and competence.
5 Act impartially and offer frank, independent advice.
6 Maintain client confidentiality.

Having established the ethical rules which advocates should apply, we must now consider the practice and skills of advocacy. At all times, the application of those skills will be guided by Principled Advocacy.

References

1 *Lord* v. *Thornton*, [1616] 80 ER 965, cited in Pannick, D. (1993), *Advocates*, Oxford University Press.
2 Kind acknowledgements to the National Association of Citizens' Advice Bureaux for permission to reproduce this policy document. The CAB updates its policies and guidance regularly. This version from February 1986.

3 Advocacy in action

This chapter shows the practice of advocacy in several welfare-related issues. Four detailed case-studies based on real-life situations illustrate the skills and practice of effective advocacy and put the earlier chapters into perspective. The situations chosen are also representative of the more common problems that are likely to confront advocates, but they are not intended to be a definitive guide to the technicalities of advocacy in different situations: rather they illustrate the types of advocacy in which advocates might find themselves engaged. Each case-study concerns advocacy in a different area: welfare rights, debt, homelessness and healthcare. The final case-study also illustrates some of the 'softer' elements of advocacy on unbounded problems concerning personal choice rather than the 'harder', quasi-legal forms of advocacy.

Welfare rights – benefiting Delia and Phillip

As I have pointed out, welfare rights work is the best-known type of advocacy on welfare issues. It is also primarily concerned with social security issues – though, inevitably, welfare rights advisers also have to develop knowledge of related matters such as housing, debt and the personal social services.

Because the social security system affects almost all citizens at some stage of their lives, it is perhaps hardly surprising that there is widespread advocacy involving social security matters. In addition, the perceptible shift towards means-testing as the main vehicle for delivery of income maintenance, the poor training and status of staff working in the social security system, and the availability of a regulated appeals system have all meant that advocacy in social security has become well-established and effective.

Two examples of the way in which advocacy on social security has become established are the ready availability of suitable reference materials and the employment of specialist welfare rights advisers in many local authorities and advice agencies. Also, the escalation of poverty in the last decade and the need for an adequate income combined with chronically low take-up rates of many benefits mean that welfare rights work is often an accepted part of the work of many people employed in the human services. Welfare rights work can become incredibly complex and require considerable specialist skills. However, it is often more straightforward. This case has elements of both simple and complex welfare rights advocacy.

Delia is a single parent with one child, Phillip, aged 5. Delia receives Income Support and lives in a flat owned by the local authority, which means that she also receives Housing and Council Tax Benefits to cover her full rent and Council Tax. Phillip has cerebral palsy, having suffered oxygen starvation at birth. He walks with difficulty and slowly, but he can make progress on foot and can walk as far as any other 5-year-old. However, his speech is indistinct and Delia is the only person who can readily understand what he says. He also needs help with toileting, washing, changing, dressing and feeding.

Delia was advised by her health visitor to apply for Disability Living Allowance, as the extra money would help with some of the extra costs of Phillip's disability and would be of considerable benefit to Delia, who cannot manage on the money she receives because benefit levels are so low. Her only income is Income Support and Child Benefit, her ex-partner is unemployed and he cannot pay any maintenance for Phillip, the relationship having broken down several years ago under the strain of caring for a severely disabled child while both were out of work.

Delia filled in an application form for Disability Living Allowance but she was turned down. Her health visitor has accompanied her to a local advice agency where she is seen by a welfare rights officer.

The first step taken by the welfare rights officer is to undertake a full check on the benefits being received. He phones the local Benefits Agency office to get a breakdown of how Delia's Income Support has been calculated. The Benefits Agency are hesitant in giving out this information and insist on ringing back the welfare rights officer to make sure that they are speaking to a bona fide adviser. The information that follows shows that Delia's Income Support has been worked out on the basis that she is a single parent with the appropriate premiums and allowances. On the face of it, this is correct. However, it appears that £3 is being deducted from her Income Support to pay off a Social Fund loan and that deductions will continue for another six weeks.

The welfare rights officer asks Delia when she received the Social Fund loan and what it was for. Delia says that the loan was taken out three months ago to buy bedding for Phillip as he had soiled and worn out his previous bedclothes. He also establishes that Delia had been notified of the refusal of Disability Living Allowance two weeks previously. The welfare rights officer takes a detailed history from Delia about Phillip's care needs and his mobility problems. He also establishes that Delia had not applied for a Social Fund *grant* as a Benefits Agency officer had told her these were very hard to get.

Before doing anything else, the welfare rights worker consults several welfare rights handbooks to check the precise wording of the legislation. In particular it is noted that for children to receive the lowest rate of Disability Living Allowance, for mobility problems, they must require substantially more help with walking than children of the same age in normal health, or that those of the same age in normal health would not need such help.

The welfare rights officer tells Delia that she ought to ask for a review of the Social Fund loan to have it converted into a Social Fund Community Care Grant – thus getting a refund of the repayments – and that she should also challenge the refusal of Disability Living Allowance. If Delia is awarded the allowance, at the right rate – there are three care rates and two for mobility – it would also increase the amount of Income Support she was entitled to, and it would trigger her right to be paid Invalid Care Allowance, which would further increase her Income Support. Delia agrees that her advocate should proceed with challenging the refusal of Disability Living Allowance and the loan deductions.

The welfare rights officer drafts two letters. One is a request for a review of the Social Fund loan, and asking that the repayments be frozen while the matter is looked into. The letter is typed out in Delia's name and it reads as follows:

Dear Sir or Madam,

I wish to have a review of my Social Fund loan. I believe that I should have been awarded a Community Care Grant as this would have eased exceptional pressure on me and my family. The loan was given for bedding for my son who has cerebral palsy and is incontinent. Frequent washing had worn out the bedding and it needed to be replaced. I am unable to afford the loan deductions from my benefit and this as well as the stress of caring for a disabled child means that the grant would ease exceptional pressure on me and my family [one of the legal criteria for a grant].

I wish to have this review dealt with outside the normal 28-day limit for review requests for the following special reasons: 1) I was misadvised by a Benefits Agency officer that it was not worth applying for a grant. I thus acted on official advice. 2) The circumstances of having a disabled child and looking after him as a single parent are out of the ordinary.

You could also choose to review outside the normal 28-day limit under Social Fund Direction 31 on the grounds that the full facts of my case were not taken into account when deciding to award a loan rather than a grant.

Please suspend deductions from my benefit while this matter is in dispute as it would be contrary to natural justice to still make deductions while a review is pending.

Please contact my representatives to arrange a convenient date and time for any review interview and also copy any papers to them. [Welfare rights officer's and health visitor's details inserted here.]

Yours faithfully

A further letter asking for a review of the refusal of Disability Living Allowance is drafted. This includes details of the tasks that Phillip is unable to do, the dangers inherent in leaving him without anyone on hand, and details of the very limited nature of his walking ability. The health visitor is asked to write a letter confirming the care needs, and she also agrees to get supporting evidence from Phillip's general practitioner and consultant. Delia is asked to keep a diary for a day listing everything she has to do for Phillip on an hour-by-hour basis. Both letters are posted.

The Social Fund loan is converted into a grant after ten days and a cheque sent refunding the deductions. The Social Fund officer decided that it was possible to review without the normal interview because facts about Phillip's disability had been overlooked. The Disability Living Allowance refusal is also reversed, and the middle rate of the care component is awarded. However, this takes over a month. Back-pay to the original date of application is sent a bit later. As the welfare rights officer has received copies of the decisions, he then writes to the local Benefits Agency asking for additional premiums to be included in Delia's Income Support. Delia also successfully claims Invalid Care Allowance, which is backdated to the same date as the Disability Living Allowance, and a further carer's premium is added to her Income Support.

This case-study illustrates the dramatic effect on a person's lifestyle when they receive appropriate advice and advocacy on benefits. It also shows the importance of independent advice – able to fulfil the ethical principles of advocacy – and it shows the value of a methodical, organised and structured approach to advocacy.

Debt – protecting Mr and Mrs Frost

The prevalence of debt is a new phenomenon. It reflects the doubling of consumer credit since 1980 and lenders' deliberate targeting of credit to those on low incomes. Combined with the almost continual tightening of many of the benefit rules and the persistence of unemployment at nearly 3 million, debt has become a sad feature of the lives of many people who use welfare services.

The aim of debt advice is to protect the interests of the debtor rather than counselling people on how to manage their money. Research confirms that the vast bulk of personal debt is not caused by reckless spending. The debt advice approach, and the necessary skills, are exemplified in the standard reference books referred to in Chapter 9. Much can be done to help the debtor where the debts are uncomplicated if the right approach is adopted. Where they are more complex, the help of a third party may be needed.

Debt advice should include:

- Income maximisation (not just *benefit* maximisation)
- Prioritisation of debts on the basis of the implications of non-payment
- Compiling a financial statement
- Selection of the best strategy for debt control
- Representing and negotiating for the debtor

Debt is one of the most serious moral issues in our society. Consequently, both creditors and debtors will bring certain perceptions and values with them. The role of the debt adviser is to avoid judgementalism, with the aim of minimising repayments to creditors by reference to objective criteria which operate in the debtor's interests. In other words, rather than seeking to evoke a positive response from the other side by making offers to pay which might be acceptable, the adviser uses a technique which demonstrates what *can* be paid. Similarly, the debt adviser is not concerned with trying to negotiate a compromise between creditor and debtor.

The skills appropriate to debt advice include the full range of advocacy skills, and there is a strong emphasis on interviewing, litigation and negotiation skills. A side effect of the debt advice approach is to steer the process while also involving the debtor and working to remove the sense of helplessness so often associated with debt. A crucial element in debt advice is the production of a financial statement. The financial statement is not a personal budget nor is it an attempt to get people to limit their expenditure. A financial statement is a document that shows objectively what money is coming in and where it goes. This is then used in negotiations and litigation to show whether there are funds available to pay debts and to form the basis of offers made to creditors.

This debt case-study concerns a not uncommon multiple-debt situation. Assume that the debtor's income has been maximised.

Mr and Mrs Frost are 45 and 46. They have two children aged 9 and 12. Mr Frost is unable to work as he suffers from chronic depression. He receives Invalidity Benefit of £135 a week. Mrs Frost works part-time and takes home £78 a week. They rent a house from the local authority and their rent is £39 a week. Because of Mr Frost's illness and the financial pressures on them, they have rent arrears of £156; the local authority has now issued them with a

Notice of Intention to Seek Possession. They also owe £3 107 to a credit company for a loan taken out some years ago to pay off other debts. They have missed several payments and interest is mounting up. In addition, their water charges for this year (£210) are unpaid and they have had a final reminder letter from the water company.

Mr and Mrs Frost have brought these matters to the attention of their social worker. The social worker has had some basic debt advice training and, together with an in-house debt adviser employed by the local authority, visits Mr and Mrs Frost to discuss the problem. The initial interview is important, so particular care is taken to reassure Mr and Mrs Frost that there is nothing immoral about debt, the visitors are there to help, not to judge, and that many people are in debt. They also need to clarify the full extent of the Frosts' indebtedness. A debtor may not reveal all their debts to an advocate – the psychological process of denial and the fact that debt is still regarded as shameful are the main reasons for this – so the initial interview needs to be as supportive as possible to enable the debtor to give full details to the advocate. Mr and Mrs Frost do in fact reveal that they have a further debt of £280 in unpaid Poll Tax from several years ago, and the council have put this debt in the hands of a bailiff. They have signed a Walking Possession Agreement (a document committing them to payments rather than having goods seized) to pay £10 a week to the bailiff.

The consequences of rent arrears are that the debtor can lose their home; non-payment of water charges can lead to disconnection, and the consequences of Poll Tax debt may ultimately be imprisonment (in England and Wales, not in Scotland), so these are priority debts. The unsecured loan is not a priority debt. These points are explained, as is the fact that a Notice of Intention to Seek Possession is a formal notice that is effectively a written warning to enable the landlord to start possession proceedings. The adviser draws up a schedule of debts, creditors' addresses, account references, and the reason for the debts. She also asks Mr and Mrs Frost to sign a written consent for their creditors to discuss matters with their advisers and for creditors to send a copy of any credit agreement they may have.

The next stage is to prepare a financial statement. It is carefully explained that this is not to set them a budget but a statement of their circumstances for use in negotiations. If the matter goes to court such information can also be very important legally, as courts will often require an understanding of the debtor's means in order to make an appropriate order. Here is Mr and Mrs Frost's financial statement.

FINANCIAL STATEMENT

NAME: Ann and Terry Frost
ADDRESS: 14 Any Street, Anytown

MEMBERS OF HOUSEHOLD:
Simon (9)
Carla (12)

WEEKLY INCOME:

Invalidity Benefit	135.00
Child Benefit	18.10
Earnings (net)	78.00
TOTAL	£231.10

WEEKLY EXPENDITURE:

Rent	39.00
Council Tax	7.74
Water charges	4.01
Insurance	4.45
Food, household items and toiletries	80.00
Electricity	9.00
Gas	5.47
Telephone	5.76
TV licence/rental	2.26
Entertainment	8.00
Furniture and bedding	3.00
Papers and magazines	4.00
School dinners	11.00
Work expenses	8.00
Travel costs	12.00
Health costs	3.00
Clothing and shoes	12.00
Pocket money	3.00
TOTAL	£221.69

Thus, there is under £10 a week available to pay debts – and that is without counting the payments towards the loan. The priority is to secure a proportional split between the priority debts and to contact the loan company to ask them to write off their debt. This strategy is suggested to the Frosts and they agree. The adviser writes to the local authority and the water company.

The local authority are reluctant to accept the offer as they say that the Frosts could pay more if they cut down on entertainment. The adviser replies pointing out that, given the family's circumstances, a modest expenditure on entertainment is important and the figure is not excessive. The offer is accepted and, in any event, the Frosts have already started paying the rent arrears at the offer rate – the landlord cannot refuse *any* payments, and the objective is to avoid further legal action by getting the arrears down and to show a good payment record.

The Poll Tax debt is difficult. The Frosts are paying a substantial sum to the bailiff's costs (or profits). The local authority are responsible for the debt and they cannot refuse any payments made. The adviser negotiates with the local authority, who are willing to accept lower payments but insist on payment going via the bailiff. The adviser resists this, but during this phase of the negotiations there are further developments.

The loan company are more resistant. They will not consider writing off the loan, refuse to freeze interest on it, and insist on their existing payments being maintained, even if doing so would result in the family having to cut into their basic standard of living. The adviser undertakes direct written negotiations on this matter but, eventually, it is decided to provoke legal action by the loan company. The Frosts then stop paying and the company issue proceedings. Even though they will incur costs and a County Court judgment against their credit record, it does mean that interest is frozen and that the court can be persuaded to set realistic repayment terms. It also has the advantage that both this debt and the old Poll Tax debt can be put onto an Administration Order, thus removing the bailiff from the equation and ensuring that any payment is at an affordable level. This is the approach taken. Mr Frost does not appear in court, and the social worker and advice worker attend with Mrs Frost to admit the loan company's claim, offering a minimal amount based on the financial statement, and also obtaining an Administration Order putting all the debts in one basket and paying them off at a level based on the spare money in the financial statement.

This case-study illustrates the ethical principles being applied – acting on instructions, keeping the client informed, acting in the client's best interest and not advising outside one's sphere of competence. It also shows the range of skills used in this type of advocacy.

Homelessness – a home for Lazlo

Advocacy for homeless people can involve some very complex legal issues. This is largely because of the current legal remedies which are available for challenging homelessness decisions, even though the main legal provisions governing homelessness are relatively straightforward and have a clear structure to be followed. There is also widespread ignorance about the law on homelessness among many advocates, as well as homeless people themselves and many of the housing officials charged with helping them.

Unsurprisingly, challenges can be made in many instances when homeless people have been refused help. Figures from the Chartered Institute of Public Finance and Accountancy show that a third of households who apply as homeless are not accepted as such.[1] Assuming that only 10 per cent of those who are refused are incorrectly refused, this represents a massive area for advocacy. The following case-study shows the application of a robust, legalistic approach in a not uncommon situation. Legally irrelevant issues – such as a person's alleged unsuitability to be a tenant – are discarded when the correct legal points are followed. The case also shows the importance of involving an expert if the matter is outside the advocate's expertise.

Lazlo is a homeless person. He came to Britain as a refugee from Hungary in the 1950s. He has experienced many spells as a psychiatric in-patient and has a chronic drink problem. He became homeless several years ago after separating from his partner. He usually stays in short-stay hostels and night shelters, but he has been in a local town for several years. His social worker is concerned about the long-term effects on his health of such a lifestyle, and has written a letter for Lazlo to take to the housing department asking that they offer him housing.

Lazlo tells her that he asked about housing at the housing department but was informed verbally that he did not qualify. His social worker mentions this and, having taken specialist advice, she asks that the department assess his housing needs as they are required to under section 62 of the Housing Act 1985 when they are approached by someone who appears to be homeless.

Lazlo's visit prompts a phone call to the social worker from the housing department. They say that they cannot possibly help this man as he is unsuitable to be a tenant; that he has accommodation because he is in a night shelter, and he is not in priority need under the Housing Act. The social worker speaks to Lazlo, who is concerned at the way he has been treated. Her next step is to write to the housing department advising that, unless they comply with the law, she will have to refer Lazlo to a solicitor. This letter is not acknowledged for two weeks.

Lazlo sees a solicitor who understands housing law. It was fortuitous that he found a solicitor who was knowledgeable about the law on homelessness. The solicitor immediately writes to the housing department's solicitors, making it clear that there has been an abject failure to perform their legal duties. First, there has not been a full assessment as required by law, as well as the provision of temporary accommodation for a person who appears to be in priority need. Second, the decision was not put in writing as required by law. Third, the facts of the case show that he is homeless within the meaning of the Act, as a night shelter is not sufficiently stable to be regarded as accommodation. He gives them 24 hours to reverse their decision.[2] He points out to the social worker that it might have been helpful to have sought his advice earlier as, in the mean time, Lazlo has had to sleep rough on several nights.

The housing department respond within a few hours and agree to assess Lazlo's needs and to provide temporary accommodation as they are required to. Lazlo moves into temporary accommodation and he is interviewed several times over the next few days about his history and needs. The housing department then write to him advising him that they now accept that he is homeless within the meaning of the legislation but that, as he is not in priority need, they are under no duty to provide permanent housing. Please can he vacate the temporary accommodation within 14 days.

The solicitor immediately initiates action in the High Court to challenge the housing department, including an injunction to force them to provide housing until the matter is dealt with. A barrister's opinion makes it clear that there are very strong chances of success and, upon taking their own legal advice, a few weeks later the housing department offer permanent accommodation.

Lazlo's case shows how effective results to meet a basic need can be achieved, provided that there is access to experts and that one is clear about the ethical obligation to act in the client's best interests.

Healthcare – meals for Michael

As has already been discussed, there are different forms of advocacy in human service organisations – the more structured, legalistic advocacy involving bounded problems, and advocacy which is reliant on assertiveness and negotiation skills for unbounded problems. The issues taken up by people such as Citizen Advocates will often be unbounded problems. Similarly, the advocacy undertaken by nurses on behalf of patients will usually involve unbounded problems. Consequently, the approach taken will be quite different to that described in the earlier case-studies.

Healthcare is an area where much is determined by the judgement of medical practitioners and other professionals. There is very little legislation to create a bounded problem – except on obvious matters such as rules of professional conduct, consent to treatment, etc. This case-study shows different skills being used by an advocate compared to those used in the other case-studies.

Francis is a Citizen Advocate for Michael. Michael has severe learning disabilities and lives in a hospital as a long-stay patient. Michael has very limited speech and can only be understood by people who know him well and who are patient with him. Generally, Michael will only talk to people he trusts. Michael has lost contact with his only remaining family, some distant relatives, and Francis was introduced as a Citizen Advocate by the hospital nursing staff. Francis's expenses are paid by the hospital and, while he is not formally managed, his local co-ordinator has her salary paid by the hospital. The hospital's financial situation is severe as they are overspent, having initially had extra funding in the first year they became a National Health Service Trust. Hospital managers have queried the value of Citizen Advocates and believe that the money supporting their activities could be spent on other areas of patient care. Several consultants share this view and believe that improvements to staff levels on the wards would be a better use of the money. The hospital's management board have recently decided that no more Citizen Advocates will be recruited and that a 'value for money' study will be undertaken within the next 12 months.

The long-term plan is for the hospital to close, so there is little incentive to spend money on refurbishment, and it is planned that Michael will eventually move out into a small hostel with four other people who have learning disabilities. However, staff at the hospital are worried that Michael's behaviour is too difficult and that he would disrupt a small group. A particular problem arises because Michael refuses to eat many meals and often ends up throwing his food at other patients. Michael likes certain foods – for example, he is very fond of sausage, chips and fried egg. It is apparent that Michael only throws food he doesn't like.

The consultant and charge nurse believe that the best response is to adopt a behaviour modification programme. This would consist of Michael not being fed after he has thrown his food and being ignored for one hour after he has done so. The hospital management have stated that it is not possible to provide a special meal for Michael. The kitchen is very old and there are no facilities for individual meals, nor are there sufficient staff employed in the kitchen to ensure that this could be done. Michael will just have to eat the same food as everyone else. The managers have tried very hard to maintain high standards of catering and are sensitive about any criticism of their efforts. The catering manager recently complained to a social worker's manager after the social worker had suggested to some visitors that there was too little variation in the meals served to patients.

Michael has eventually confided in Francis that he hates much of the hospital's food. He knows it is wrong to throw his food but he won't eat food he doesn't like. Francis has compiled a list of all the food that Michael says he likes. At Michael's next case review Francis suggests that, rather than trying to get Michael to adjust to the external world, the world should be more sensitive to Michael's needs. This would best be achieved by serving foods that Michael likes. There is considerable opposition to this. It is felt that not only would this be impracticable given the hospital's financial situation but the way that the catering department is organised would not accommodate one-off meal requests. The consultant thinks that this would be the worst possible solution as it would merely reinforce to Michael that he can get his own way by behaving anti-socially. This is not in his interests and only prolongs his stay in the hospital, as he cannot move out until the problem with tantrums at mealtimes has been resolved.

Francis decides that little will be achieved by negotiating further at this stage. There is no charter for the patients setting out issues of choice of food, and the level of opposition is so high that change is impossible without careful tactics. However, he does make it clear that Michael is unlikely to react well to the proposed behaviour modification programme, and that the hospital might be in hot water if it were to emerge that they had effectively denied food to a patient. The case review decides to proceed with the programme, but only when written guidelines have been drawn up by the charge nurse and consultant after discussions with the hospital's chief executive.

Francis visits the hospital's accountant. He discusses the problem and learns that to have a member of the catering staff prepare a special meal for Michael – and one would be needed 85 per cent of the time as Michael only likes 15 per cent of the standard meals on offer – would cost an additional 60 minutes of two catering staff members' time. An additional £300 would have to be spent on a cooker. The cost of the behaviour modification programme is 75 minutes of two nursing staff's time, as well as the cost of damage and extra laundry each time there is a food-throwing incident. The additional costs of Michael taking up a place in hospital for a longer time are substantial but hard to assess. It is clearly cheaper to prepare food that Michael likes.

Francis asks the consultant to hold a further case review so that the food-throwing can be discussed again. This is agreed. Francis makes a clear and assertively put case for special meals for Michael. He is clear about what appeals to the other side, and negotiates on the basis of everyone winning something rather than defeating the other side. If Michael were to have special meals, he could gradually be encouraged to try other foods. Indeed, Francis says that Michael has told him that he will try a new bit of food each week provided that he has food he likes the rest of the week. Francis is also willing to work out a weekly menu with Michael which could be given to the kitchen staff to help their planning. The cost of the extra meals is such that, on strict economic grounds, it is a winner. Francis says that if the hospital's chief executive could be persuaded to use some of the budget set aside for the closure programme this would be the way to finance the meals, and it would be a legitimate use of the money as Michael would be able to move into the hostel sooner. Michael wants to move into the hostel as soon as possible, as he has seen some of the new hostels that other patients have moved into, and they are much nicer than the hospital: he would have his own room rather than a cubicle on a ward. Francis points out that he is very conscious of the pressures on the catering staff, and that he would be happy to see the catering manager with the charge nurse to discuss the importance of the special meals.

The case review agrees to Francis's proposal. He is pleased, as he was unsure what to do if they did not agree and went ahead with the behaviour modification programme. The review decides that the special meals will be tried for one month to see what effect this has on Michael's behaviour. If there is a distinct reduction in the food-throwing incidents, the behaviour modification will not proceed.

A week later Francis and the charge nurse visit the catering manager to discuss the issue. The funding for the extra staff time and the cooker have been agreed by the chief executive after an approach by the consultant. The manager is easily persuaded to organise the special meals on a trial basis as he knows that the chief executive is backing the programme, and Francis makes a point of praising the catering department's efforts to offer high-quality food. Francis provides a list of the food that Michael likes as a further gesture of co-operation. The next week the special meals start. The food-throwing incidents all but disappear and Michael is persuaded by Francis that he must now keep to his promise to try one new food each week.

The special meals were so successful that Michael was able to move out of the hospital within seven months. He now lives in a small hostel and is helped by the staff there to cook whatever meals he chooses. However, the hospital still decided to conduct their 'value for money' study of Citizen Advocates.

This example of advocacy is very different to the other three in this chapter. It is an example of advocacy on a problem where creative and non-threatening approaches are needed, rather than the robust, quasi-legal approach on bounded problems. There is a strong emphasis on inter-personal skills and negotiation. However, a basic ethical commitment to the client is still required if the objective jointly agreed with the client is to be achieved.

References

1 Chartered Institute of Public Finance and Accountancy (1993), *Homelessness Statistics 1991/92*.
2 See *R* v. *Waveney District Council ex p. Bowers* [1993] 15 HLR 118.

Part II

The advocate's skills

4 Introduction to Part II

Unlike most other areas of activity undertaken by people working in human service organisations, there are almost no short courses on the skills needed for advocacy, few books are available on the subject, and it is often not considered in depth on basic training courses for nurses, social workers and housing staff. This situation is absurd. As discussed earlier, advocacy has been most highly developed in the welfare rights field, but the highly structured, regulated social security system has meant that technical knowledge of the minutiae of social security law has been seen as more important than advocacy skills. While personality and technical knowledge influence the advocate's effectiveness, a thorough grounding in the process of advocacy and the negotiation and tactical skills it involves are just as important – if not more so.

Advocates who have no legal training can take comfort from the fact that the lack of recognition of advocacy as a skill has not been peculiar to human service professions. Both the Law Society and the Bar Council have changed their professional courses so that budding solicitors and barristers are able to act and advocate properly. It was previously assumed that legal advocates would learn reams of written law and somehow absorb practical skills at the expense of their clients. These courses now include substantial practical elements and there is an emphasis on inter-personal skills which in past years was absent. Even the legal profession has acknowledged that technical skill is not everything.

The driving force behind the use of advocacy skills is the advocate's ethical stance. If the advocate is being effective in a human service setting, the code of ethics set out in Chapter 2 will form the building blocks for any successful advocacy, and will ultimately determine which skills are used in advocacy and the commitment with which they are applied.

Part II concentrates on a range of skills needed by advocates. Many readers may already be using these, and some will be familiar to others. The skills will relate directly to the ethics described in Chapter 2, and they will also reflect the stages of advocacy described in Chapter 11. Each chapter in this section covers a specific skill and explores the range of competences and activity which make up the core skills of successful advocacy.

The advocate's core skills

- Interviewing
- Assertiveness
- Negotiation
- Self-management
- Legal research
- Litigation

5 Interviewing

Advocacy starts in the office. It often starts with an interview, and interviewing will be the main method of obtaining instructions and for keeping clients informed. Interviews may not always be carried out face to face: it can be perfectly feasible to undertake them by telephone though, in the case of many people on low incomes, you will need to make the call rather than them because of the cost.

Interviewing is a skill common to many professions and situations. It is the interface between the organisation and its service users. Poor interviewing will lead to unclear instructions, and this can mean not only that advocates exceed their brief, but that there is a lack of clarity about the facts of a case. Much poor practice arises from inadequate interviewing, so this is a skill which advocates must get right, and one which they should constantly try to improve. Advocates must be aware of their interviewing style and its strengths and weaknesses.

In Chapter 11 I describe the six stages of advocacy. The second of these stages is information-gathering and the fourth is interpretation and feedback. During both of these stages, interviewing and interviewing skills are used extensively, and they enable advocates to obtain the information needed to make a judgement about tactics and to advise the client while acting in their best interests.

There are certain distinguishing features of an interview: an interview is a conversation with a purpose. It has, rather self-evidently, been described as having a beginning, a middle and an end. An interview should thus have a clear structure. It is not just an interesting way to pass the time.

Spot the interview

Identify the last discussion you had with a client. Where was:

1   The beginning?
2   The middle?
3   The end?

What was the purpose of each part of the discussion?
If you can't identify the basic structure, and your purpose for the discussion was unclear, was it really an interview?

The social work profession has done much to develop interviewing as a skill, and Jamieson listed ten principles of interviewing which provide useful guidance for interviews by advocates:

Jamieson's rules

1   Try to tell the interviewee how much time is available for the interview. No specific time is optimum, though five minutes is probably too short and over an hour too long.
2   Start where the client is. Explain to him why he is being seen, or, if he asked to see you, ask him why.
3   Try to have sympathy for the client, however unsympathetic a person he may be. The aim must be to make the client relaxed and unafraid.
4   Try to have empathy with the client – to see things through his eyes.
5   Do not be judgemental or condemnatory. Try to show acceptance and tolerance.
6   Smile on first acquaintance. This may help the client to communicate more freely.
7   Do not ask questions that can be answered simply 'yes' or 'no'.
8   Do not put answers into the client's mouth.
9   It is inappropriate to probe too deeply . . . and it is wrong to probe deeply at all unless there is a clear purpose in doing so.
10   Don't be afraid of silences . . . but don't prolong silences when to do so would be felt as an uncomfortable and even aggressive act on the part of the interviewer.[1]

Within the interview, there are a range of skills which the advocate will use. These include:

- Listening
- Questioning

- Understanding non-verbal aspects
- Recording
- Cultural sensitivity
- Feeding back

Listening

Listening has been described as an art form. Good listening skills are needed so that advocates do not impose their version of events on interviews. It is also very important on a simple, practical level because poor listening can lead to insufficient gathering of facts, and errors of judgement about the tactics to be employed.

There are many things which act as a barrier to effective listening. Some of them are internal, some are external. Some will be easy to address, others less easy. The main thing is to start developing an awareness of the barriers to effective listening. By developing an awareness of your own barriers you will become a better interviewer, as you will then subconsciously work to address the problems.

Barriers to listening

Here is a list of common barriers to effective listening. Tick how many apply to yourself. Add up to four more barriers of your own at the end of the list. Then go back over the list and put a cross by the ones which you personally can do something about.

External barriers

Interviewing in a room which is:

- Too noisy
- Too cold
- Too hot
- Too crowded
- So small that you are too close to the client
- Dirty or smelly
- Too dark

Being interrupted by:

- Phones
- Deliveries

- Clients calling without an appointment
- Your boss
- Colleagues dropping in to see you

Being distracted by:

- Things on your desk
- Overheard conversations outside
- Funny noises or shapes on the computer screen next to you

Concentrating on:

- The client's clothing
- The client's physical appearance
- The client's way of speaking or unusual expressions
- Your own appearance

Internal barriers

- Feeling tired
- Feeling in a hurry
- Bias
- Not liking the client or their views
- Ignoring non-verbal elements
- Boredom

List four others:

_____

_____

_____

_____

There are a number of simple things that you can do to improve your listening skills and thus the success rate of your advocacy – measures such as closing the door, interviewing in private, diverting phone calls if interviewing face to face, adjusting the heating and organising your work so that you are not under so much stress will be a good start.

Other measures include:

- Prepare yourself mentally to listen, and remind yourself, both at the outset and throughout the interview, that you must listen.

- Adopt an open posture. Don't interview with your arms folded across your chest.
- Come out from behind your desk.
- Follow the flow of ideas being put across by the client.
- Resist the impulse to rush into advising the client. This can come later.

However, perhaps the greatest barriers to good listening include fear of silences and the desire to repeat our learned behaviour in social conversations. Interviewing is part of a formal activity so there is no need to speak just to pass the time of day.

Cutting off a client who is being silent is likely to distract them from saying something significant. It will also stop you from concentrating on what has been said to you. It could also lead you into questioning about wholly irrelevant areas, so wasting yours and the client's time, as well as meaning that you may fail to gather facts which are critical to the success of the client's case. If this happens, you could have to do more work and face some embarrassment in contacting the client again for the information not obtained earlier.

There are often situations where the client digresses onto subjects that are not directly relevant to the issue or which are irrelevant. Careful listening will ensure that you are not led off on a mental by-way, and you will be able to steer the discussion back to the main issue. Lack of listening will make it easier to be diverted onto futile irrelevancies.

By honing your listening skills, it should be possible to engage in what has been described as 'active listening'.

Active listening

An exercise to improve listening skills

Switch on a television programme. Sit facing the screen. Listen carefully to what is being said for five minutes. Also, video the five-minute clip. Then write down the salient points of what was said. Compare your notes to the video-taped version. What did you miss? Why?

Repeat the exercise while making a cup of tea, playing with children or having someone else talk at you.

Another exercise

Find a partner. Ask them to describe to you what they did yesterday. While doing so, make notes of what they say. Ensure that you are sitting facing them, leaning forward slightly, and that you nod or 'grunt' approvingly at gaps in the conversation. Then feed back to your partner what they have said. How accurate was your listening?

Questioning

Asking the right question at the right time is essential both for effective interviewing and effective advocacy. Because facts are the building blocks of fine advocacy, the questions must relate to the facts which are relevant and can also help steer the interview in the right direction. Effective questioning goes hand in hand with effective listening.

Questioning as part of advocacy has a different function than in other types of interviews in human service organisations. An interview in other settings may be, for example, an integral part of a therapeutic process, in which direct questioning may be discouraged and more emphasis put on a non-directive approach. However, questioning must be sensitive and related to the ethics of advocacy. It is especially important to be sensitive to the power relationship between many advocates and their clients. Advocates in human service organisations will often have greater power and influence over the life of the client than they may imagine. Even if the power and influence are not real, they are perceived as such by many clients; given the negative experiences of many people in their dealings with the welfare state, any questioning may be seen as intrusive and irrelevant by a client. Therefore, the first rule of questioning is to explain to the client *why* you are asking the question.

The second rule is to use indirect questions. Much can be achieved by reflecting back to the client something that they have just said – for example, 'So you say that he told you that you could not be considered as homeless?' This can help the client to clarify their thoughts, and it helps you to see the facts from a slightly different perspective, or to ascertain further facts which are relevant. Similarly, nods, smiles and 'grunts' can be used to help the flow of information from the client. A conventional, direct question may not be necessary and could interrupt things at a vital stage. Reflecting things back to the client also means that both parties have a common understanding of important facts.

The third rule is to ask the right type of question at the right time. This means the selective use of closed and open questions. An open question is one which is designed to produce a range of answers. Open questions help the client to expand upon what they have said and so help you to see the wider picture. They can also produce significant additional information. Examples of an open question would be:

- 'What did the housing officer say to you when you said you were homeless?'
- 'How do you manage to live on your money?'
- 'What can you tell me about your health?'

A range of answers could be given to these questions. They also enable the client to feel more in control of the questioning process, but they could lead to your being bombarded with facts and to the interview straying off into irrelevancies. Open questions will tend to produce open answers.

Closed questions are ones which will tend to produce restricted or closed answers. They are useful to pull an interview back on track or to focus on precise information. The answers to closed questions will often consist of just one or two words. Over-use of closed questions can be hard work for both advocate and client, can slow down the gathering of information, and can lull you into a false sense of security in believing that you have all the necessary facts when, in reality, you don't. It may appear to be quicker to direct an interview by asking many closed questions. In the long run it is often slower, and is likely to make your advocacy less effective and less rewarding.

Examples of closed questions include:

- 'Did the housing officer tell you that they could not give you permanent accommodation?'
- 'Do you receive Income Support?'
- 'How often do you have dizzy spells?'

What type of question?

In the following scenarios, indicate whether a closed or an open question should be used to move the interview in a direction where facts can be gathered.

1   A client tells you that they need somewhere else to live as their partner is being violent towards them.
2   You are trying to establish from a client whether or not all their social security benefits are correct – you think that they are underclaiming. The client has already said that they get £67 a week and you know that their health is poor.
3   A client who is facing disciplinary action by his employer has just said that he admits that he assaulted a fellow employee but that the employee had made racist remarks about him to his face.
4   A client whose benefit cheque has not turned up has already said that it was expected yesterday, and has reported it to the police, Post Office and DSS. You don't know what benefit they are on or how much.

Understanding non-verbal aspects

Interviewing is as much about what is not said as about what is said. We all communicate both verbally and non-verbally. Much of an advocate's work may be undertaken via the telephone. In such cases it will be far harder to pick up on non-verbal aspects of the interview.

Much has been written about the importance of non-verbal communication and I don't want to repeat all that has been said elsewhere but, as it is the main way in which we emphasise or contradict what we say, it is necessary to mention some of the more important aspects.

Perhaps the most common non-verbal aspect of an interview by an advocate is the embarrassment felt by the client. As non-verbal communication is affected by personality, this will display itself in many ways – the common signs are blushing, evasive eye contact or silence. Lack of sensitivity by the advocate to embarrassment can undermine the contact between advocate and client to such an extent that the client decides to withdraw instructions. And, as many of the subjects which advocates are involved in – poverty, bad housing, debt, services from the health services – all involve very personal aspects of people's lives, there is likely to be embarrassment at just discussing these issues.

The growth of poverty in the last decade has heightened the sense of isolation of those on low incomes as society becomes more competitive and success as a person is equated with personal wealth. Far from creating a sense of solidarity and collectivism, the growth of poverty can mean that it is more difficult for people to disclose their penury. Even questioning about a client's financial situation needs careful handling, and clues should be picked up from non-verbal aspects of the interview.

The following are the most useful non-verbal clues to be aware of in an interview:

- Distance between advocate and client
- Eye contact
- Silence

Distance

Keep the appropriate physical distance between the client and yourself. Being too physically close to the client invades their privacy and makes it more difficult for them to respond to questions – especially where the subject matter might be embarrassing. This has implications for the layout of interview facilities. (It never ceases to amaze me how small and cramped many interview facilities are.) If interviewing in a person's home, physical distance can be smaller, as being on the client's territory makes it less threatening for them to discuss matters. This could influence your choice of venue, though the value of a home visit needs to be weighed against the time and cost involved.

However, don't put too much distance between you and the client. As a rule of thumb, research has found a distance of 1.5 to 2 metres between interviewer and interviewee to be most comfortable.[2] This may have to be increased if one person is large or threatening, and can be decreased when the people involved feel comfortable with each other and the issues being discussed. There are no hard and fast rules – simply be aware of the importance of distance.

Finally, as interviews are usually conducted when seated, sitting positions are also important. Sitting side by side along a table is more likely to facilitate equality and eliciting better instructions from the client than sitting across a table, which can impose a barrier to effective communication. It is also important to make sure that chairs are of a similar height – and that people with disabilities can get in and out of the chairs provided.

Eye contact

Much research has been done on the importance of eye contact. People tend to exhibit longer eye gazes when listening. It is useful to note that, when giving advice, lack of good eye contact may mean that your advice is not being absorbed. Your own eye contact will also give out such messages. People also look less frequently at people if they dislike them, and when they are uncomfortable or are lying. Normal human interaction is usually started with a long gaze followed by intermittent eye contact.

In one experiment, it was found that when given constant eye contact and reinforcement by an interviewer, interviewees relaxed and spoke more freely. When eye contact was refused, interviewees lapsed into embarrassed silence.

Silence

I have already mentioned the importance of not rushing to fill the silences in an interview. They play an important role in enabling interviewees to feel their way and to articulate difficult matters. There are also people who are less forthcoming, and silence is just their way of punctuating speech. Silence may also be a sign of anxiety, as speech becomes broken up when we are anxious. There are also cultural aspects to silence. For example, it has been suggested in research that middle-class people tend to use silences more than working-class people, so that more sensitivity to the role of silence in conversations will be needed with some people.[3]

Recording

Keeping a written record of advocacy can be tedious, and may be seen as a time-consuming distraction from the main task of getting results for the client. Many advocates will have to keep written records of their non-advocacy work, so they will find it more natural to commit things to paper.

Written records must fit the purpose for which they are intended. Too much time can be spent writing up details of contacts with clients for its own sake, or out of fear that one may be called to account for some minor misdemeanour.

The purposes of written records in advocacy are as follows:

- To act as an *aide-mémoire.*
- To record facts which are relevant to the case.
- To ensure accountability and to give an indication of the workload involved in a piece of advocacy.
- To enable another advocate to step in if you are not available.
- To ensure that the client can obtain justice if the advocate has overlooked something or made a mistake.
- If records are to be open to clients, to show your understanding of the situation.
- If well-designed, to help advocates manage their time better.
- To help managers assess a service's effectiveness and cost.
- To contribute to the greater understanding of advocacy and social issues. Records can be kept and then researched in later years by historians – how limited our understanding of the horrors of the Poor Law would be if no one had kept records of how it was administered.

In any event, all advocates will collect large quantities of documentation about clients. Letters are written to the other side, appeals undertaken and even litigation commenced. All of these can involve substantial amounts of written work and it will always be necessary to have an effective filing and retrieval system. Written accounts of the advocate's work should be kept in the same place and could be in the form of a running record.

Recording can take several forms. The records may be in the shape of rough notes taken during an interview. It is especially important to record precise data such as income figures, dates, health problems, etc. These may then be transferred onto some form of summary sheet as set out in the box opposite.

SUMMARY SHEET

Names (First) ....

(Last) ....

DOB ....

National Insurance No. ....

Address ....

....

Postcode ....

Family details:

Name	Relationship	DOB

Health details:

....

....

....

....

....

GP ....

Consultant ....

Landlord's name and address:

....

....

....

....

Income details:

Earnings (Net pw)

....

Benefits received – name and amount

....

....

....

Advocates may also find that they write formal reports on a client for other purposes. It may be appropriate to use these in advocacy. A running record of events in a case will help you or a colleague to see quickly what is happening, and an action sheet may be useful in helping you to work out tactics in a case. There is no ideal method of recording. The key considerations are that it should be recognised as being important and that a consistent method is used and reviewed regularly to assess whether or not it meets the needs of both advocate and client.

It is tempting to treat written records on a client as your own personal property. In law they belong to the employer, and good practice should dictate that they are open to the client. This will raise all the usual dilemmas about who should have access to records, which information is very sensitive and which was given in confidence, etc. One way forward is to be clear from the outset about what records are kept and who has access to them. Similarly, clients need to be involved in record-keeping. The simple act of taking notes on a special form which are then read back to the client with the understanding that these are the records of the case will ensure that the process is democratic and participative. Similarly, good practice would dictate that the client is sent copies of correspondence from the other side as a case progresses.

Given the ethical principles that advocates should act on a client's instructions, act in their best interests and observe rules of confidentiality, you must not record your personal views of the client. It would be fair to record an assessment of the chances of success of a case, but it is not acceptable to record personal feelings. The record must be purely factual. It must also be brief enough not to be a burden, while being long enough to enable someone else to see what has happened, what has been done and what needs to be done. The nature of advocacy is such that existing recording methods in organisations may not be appropriate. There is thus a strong argument for a unique method of recording for advocates.

Putting the record straight

Write a brief factual summary of your last contact with a client. The record must conform to the following rules:

1   It must be accurate.
2   It must not be more than 250 words long.
3   It must contain no comments about the client, their views, their appearance, culture or the justice of their case.
4   It must summarise the facts of the case and highlight those which appear to particularly favour their cause.

Then show this record to the client and ask for their views.

Cultural sensitivity

The ethical principles of advocacy mean that advocates need to be objective about the situations they deal with, but objectivity must not be an excuse for not taking account of the cultural aspects of a situation and the ways in which culture can influence interaction between advocate and client, thus influencing instructions, actions on behalf of a client and the final outcome of a case.

'Culture' is a misused word. It can mean customs and habits, and it can also refer to the attributes of a society or group. At its crudest it has connotations of ethnic art and music. In a sociological sense, 'culture' means shared values and norms. There is much research and anecdotal evidence to influence us in developing more sensitivity to cultural aspects of work with other people. Several key issues emerge in the importance of developing cultural sensitivity. Cultural sensitivity is most acute in the process of interviewing, and it is here that the ethical principles of advocacy are most likely to be undermined.

Cultural issues can emerge in a number of ways:

- In verbal and non-verbal communication
- In attitudes towards issues
- In how much control the advocate should exercise over the client
- In how directive the advocate should be in their advice-giving
- In the different emphasis placed on the meaning of words used by client and advocate

The most common cultural differences may arise as a result of differences in gender, race and class between advocate and client. The overriding rule in cultural sensitivity is to be aware that such differences exist and may be present in a given situation, affecting communication and interpretation of what is said. Such differences are very likely to be encountered by advocates in human service organisations. Advocates are likely to have considerably greater economic power than clients and will frequently be formally educated to a higher level. If the advocate has a senior position within an organisation, they are also more likely to be male, white, Anglo-Saxon Protestants, which may not be true of the client.

Cultural clashes can also occur between advocates and the other side, or may explain the responses towards clients from the other side. For example, problems such as chronic poverty and the way in which people on low incomes have to constantly juggle their finances in order to survive can produce debts and broken agreements to repay them. The other side, if a creditor, may not see the issue in such terms and may view the non-payment as arising out of fecklessness or duplicity. Such a lack of understanding is a symptom of class differences and the way in which personal values often reflect personal income and economic position.

Race and gender differences can produce significant distortions in communication, and sometimes outright prejudice from the other side. Sadly, it is not unknown for the other side to behave in a racist or sexist manner, or for assumptions about the client to be related to their gender or ethnic group.

Cultural sensitivity is thus an important element of acting within ethical principles, as well as a skill to be developed on a personal level.

It is, of course, also important to develop specific and appropriate interviewing skills for people with learning disabilities or mental health difficulties, and for children. Very careful attention will be needed here, and particular care will be needed to devise methods of communication which they can relate to, and which do not reinforce traditional roles of 'helper' and 'victim'.

Feeding back

Feeding back to the client is questioning in reverse. It is especially important when you have reached a stage in your advocacy where you have to share conclusions with a client or where they want to reflect upon their version of events. It is important to develop an honest and open relationship with a client, in which there is trust, so a degree of sensitivity may be required when feeding back to a client. Feeding back also enables you to check that your understanding of what was said is correct. Effectively, it acts as a safety check on your listening skills.

There is also a distinct stage in the advocacy process where you feed back to the client the results of any technical or other research undertaken, together with an opinion about the tactics and prospects. This is to ensure that the client is involved in matters, and also to enable you to obtain better instructions. As with questioning, the language used must be appropriate, using plain English and avoiding obscure or technical terms.

Feedback exercise

Find a partner to practise with, then ask them to summarise, for at least four minutes, the football results in a newspaper. Listen to what they are saying and then, when your partner has finished, feed back in plain English what you understand the football results were. Your partner should then check how accurate your version is.

Conclusion

Interviewing is an important ingredient in the mix of skills needed in advocacy. It will form the basis of much information-gathering and for establishing important facts to strengthen the client's case. It includes a broad range of skills, and they are all applied during interviewing so that it may fulfil the requirements for the advocate to act for the client within the principles of advocacy set out in Chapter 2.

References

1 Jamieson, J. (1978), 'What is an Interview?', *Community Care*, 8 February, cited in Davies, M., op. cit.
2 For example, see Sommer, R. (1969), *Personal Space*, Englewood Cliffs, NJ: Prentice-Hall; and Hall, E.T. (1969), *The Hidden Dimension*, New York: Doubleday.
3 Dohrenwend, B. and Chin-Shong, E. (1967), 'Social Status and Attitudes towards Psychological Disorder: The Problem of Tolerance of Deviance', *American Sociological Review*, **32**: 417–33.

6 Assertiveness and the constructive use of aggression

Advocates must be assertive. Advocates who aren't assertive will always find advocacy difficult, and will be less effective. Assertion as a skill has been more associated with social or group situations. However, there are elements of it which are relevant to advocacy – especially where one is advocating about an unbounded problem where there is no regulated structure against which to frame one's actions.

Being assertive means expressing oneself in a direct, honest and non-manipulative way, as opposed to aggressive or – at the other extreme – submissive behaviour. It also involves not violating the rights of those people one is asserting against – however, there is a tension with the need to act in the client's best interests, which may involve having to be exceptionally assertive to defend or secure their rights. Advocates also face the added problem of the other side becoming defensive merely because someone is asserting the rights of a service user or is challenging or querying their judgement.

In advocacy, assertion on its own may not be enough. The advocate may also have to be vigorous in being prepared to carry out the ultimate sanctions to support a client's case. This need not be done unpleasantly, but it may be necessary to make clear to the other side what the consequences of their actions could be. It goes without saying that, if this is done, the advocate must be prepared to ensure that such sanctions are carried out.

Assertion was one of the qualities which Kahn identified as characterising effective advocates in human service organisations. Other qualities and traits identified by Kahn are: advocates are likely to be natural leaders with strong personalities and expertise in their subject; they are knowledgeable and get their facts right; they are politically adept, known for their professional integrity and capable of presenting a client's case forcefully and efficiently. People who need frequent reassurance or consultation with

77

colleagues tend not to be good advocates. According to Kahn, advocates are also more self-reliant and autonomous than others.[1]

Such qualities are all associated with assertiveness. Lack of the right range of assertiveness skills is likely to mean that the advocate is deflected by the other side. The other side will be seeking to defend their position or interests as much as the advocate will be asserting the position of the client. However pleasantly or reasonably the other side puts their case for not granting what- ever the advocate is seeking, their primary motivation may be to defend their position or resources. As part of their ethical duties, the advocate may have no alternative but to carry out actions which force the other side to give way. This is more likely when dealing with bounded problems, and it is thus not surprising that advocacy on legal issues often consists of threats, defences and counter-claims in an attempt to obtain a win for one side. It is not possible, whatever the type of problem, to comply with the ethical duty to act on instructions and in the client's best interests if there is no assertion.

It is almost inevitable – especially if the advocate's proposition affects the financial or organisational interests of the other side – that some resistance will be met. The resistance will be intensified if the other side also hold nega- tive views about the client or the client's lifestyle. Similarly, when the other side is a bureaucracy, the staff in such organisations can develop defensive cultures or behaviour (such as not responding to correspondence) as a result of working with insufficient resources, or for other reasons. In such cases, having to respond to a challenge, in the short term, takes up more time. In cases involving unbounded problems a more imaginative process involving negotiation skills is likely to be more effective than the vigorous approach used on bounded problems. However, negotiation will require assertiveness and the ability to communicate your goals clearly and calmly.

As with other advocacy skills, it is often assumed that assertiveness is a personality trait which people either do or do not have. The fact that some people are naturally more assertive than others only reinforces this. However, like most inter-personal skills, assertiveness can be enhanced with the right support, training and feedback. Similarly, having a good grasp of the relevant facts and a good grasp of the technical, legal and policy issues involved will help you to feel more assertive and confident in putting your clients' cases.

In Chapter 11 I describe the stages of advocacy. Recognising those stages and applying the appropriate skills at particular stages will automatically make you more confident and assertive, and so better able to act for your client.

How assertive are you?

Go through the following list. Mark a score of 1 to 5 against each type of situation. 5 is the highest and means that you feel wholly confident in such a situation and are able to persuade the other side of the rightness of your case and to achieve the objective you set out with. 1 is the lowest and means that you have little confidence in your ability to persuade in such a situation, and you know that you will not achieve anything other than perhaps feeling rejected or frustrated.

1   You phone the council to persuade them not to evict a client who has rent arrears of £1 000. The client has a small child and has persistently broken agreements to pay off the debt. However, she is in poor health and the arrears arose because the council made a mess of her Housing Benefit when she tried working in a low-paid job for a few months. You suspect that the figures for the rent arrears are wrong. The housing department's staff have previously told you that they think the client is 'a waster', there are plenty of homeless people who want her house who *will* pay the rent, so they aren't bothered if she is evicted.

2   You buy a vacuum cleaner and four months later a part falls off. You take it back to the shop. The shop manager refuses a refund because you did not keep the receipt, and she says that you must have misused the vacuum cleaner for this type of damage to occur. You know this is wrong. The manager is an articulate middle-class woman in her fifties.

3   You order 300 kilos of coal by phone and it is delivered to your home when you are out. When you inspect it in your bunker, you find that the supplier has delivered the wrong type of coal and you can't use it in your fireplace without breaking the clean air legislation. You phone the supplier, who refuses to consider a refund because he clearly remembers you ordering house coal and this is what was written on the order form. The supplier is a man who sounds gruff and irritable. You paid for the coal by credit card when you ordered over the phone.

4   Your partner wants to go out to the cinema but you want to stay at home and do some reading for an important job interview the next day. Your partner says that you always want to stay at home, that you are selfish and that you won't get the job anyway.

5   A senior manager calls you into the office and says that he is concerned about your timekeeping. You were late to work three times this week and twice the previous week. If there is any repeat of this pattern he will deal with it formally. This is a new job, you were unemployed for nine months beforehand and jobs are hard to get. This is a well-paid, interesting job, but you feel that the senior manager's tone is unpleasant and the criticism is unjustified as you were only late twice this week and it is because you have got out of the habit of getting up early. Before you have a chance to tell him all of this, the manager says he is not interested in listening to excuses.

6   A member of the public comes to the office just as it is closing. They want to see someone to talk about something which you feel is not urgent. It is Friday afternoon, you've had a bad week and want to get to the nursery to collect your daughter. The member of the public is aggressively insisting that they see someone as it is inconvenient for them to come back at another time and you know that it will take half an hour to hear them out.

7   Having got rid of the above caller you are just walking out of the office when you are approached by a polite, elderly woman who wants to see someone about something which you know will only take two minutes to resolve. She says that she has spent the last hour and a half on the bus in freezing cold weather and she can't afford the fare.

Your total score   _____

This is hardly a scientific test, but it will give you an indication about the situations where you feel more confident and assertive. However, if you have scored consistently high points, you may need to consider if you are over-asserting yourself unnecessarily to the point of aggression. If you scored consistently low points, you may want to consider if you are being too submissive.

There is no optimum level of assertiveness. Each situation and problem faced by an advocate will require a particular style to resolve successfully. The first situation described in the above exercise may require a more persistent response and, if this did not work, active steps would have to be taken to safeguard the client's rights as this is a case where there are significant legal and quasi-legal aspects which could be used to defend the client's position. The two cases involving returning goods to a supplier also involve the law but are unlikely to require as strong an approach as the first. Citing the law and making threats to one's partner in the fourth example are unlikely to result in a satisfactory outcome for anyone. So the level of resolution and assertion will always depend on a number of variables.

The variables which will affect both the style needed and the confidence that you feel will include:

- Your personal commitment to the cause or the client.
- The way in which you react to particular individuals acting for the other side.
- The way in which people may become more resolute when they meet resistance.
- The importance of the issue for the client. You may be less concerned with a technical breach of the law on clean air than with the loss of someone's home. Someone committed to green issues will feel stronger about clean air than someone who is not committed.
- The technical and legal knowledge you have about the issue.
- The level of support and the perceived level of support that you may have from superiors.
- The influence that the other side may have on your superiors.
- The vulnerability of the other side to a successful challenge.
- Your knowledge that you or a colleague have successfully advocated in similar situations in the past.
- The other side's knowledge that you have won cases in the past: your credibility.

Improving assertiveness skills

There are a number of established texts on assertiveness skills and short courses are also available. Certain aspects of established assertiveness training are particularly useful. For example, the exercise known as 'Stuck Record', set out in the box below, is based on an exercise commonly known as 'Broken Record'. This is an exercise which you can practise with a friend or colleague. It highlights the importance of assertiveness in pursuit of rights and the need to act resolutely and persistently. Persistence is often needed when the other side procrastinate, prevaricate or if they ignore you.

Stuck record

You have bought some Corsican cheese from a local shop. On getting home and opening the package, you find that there are maggots in the cheese. The next day you take the cheese back to the shop and ask for a refund. It is a busy shopping day and the shop is crowded. The shopkeeper appears to be impatient. You have often shopped here as there is an interesting range of products which are normally of good quality. Your partner should take the part of the shopkeeper.

You: 'I bought this cheese yesterday. When I got home and opened it, I found it was full of maggots ... [at this point add a phrase of your choice asking for a refund].'

Shopkeeper: 'Well this sort of Corsican cheese always has maggots. It adds to the flavour and it is a local delicacy. You should have known this when you bought it. Anyway, the maggots are quite harmless.'

You: [Respond by pointing out that you would prefer to have your money back, that there was no mention of maggots on the label and you really can't stomach the thought of eating cheese with maggots in.]

Shopkeeper: 'Well as I say, the cheese is supposed to have maggots in it. You wouldn't expect me to refund money to anyone who finds that they don't like the taste of exotic foodstuffs. I'd soon be out of business and it's hard enough trying to run a shop as it is.'

You: [Respond by repeating your request to have your money back.]

Shopkeeper: 'Look I'm very busy. Can't you see that you're holding up everyone else who wants to be served. I'm just not prepared to give you your money back.'

You: [Repeat, again, your request to have your money back. Do not add anything else at this stage.]

Shopkeeper: 'Oh very well, as you're a regular customer I'll give you a refund. How much did you say it was? £1.27?'

Commentary

It can be very effective to continue to repeat your request, calmly and clearly. It is a form of behaviour which the other side may not expect, so there may be

---

attempts to circumvent by emotional manipulation (e.g. the point about how hard it is to run a shop). Your opening remarks can set the scene. How did you phrase your request? Was it a loud demand to have an instant refund (over-assertive) or a meek, submissive, questioning request about money (non-assertive)? How far could the use of logic (e.g. the points you made about the maggots) have been used? Would a threat to take your custom elsewhere have been more effective? If such a threat had been made, would you really have wanted to go elsewhere (assuming there is a suitable alternative place to go to)? Would your approach have been different if, instead of being an interesting local shop, it had been a branch of a supermarket chain?

Threats and aggression

Some advocates – usually where the problem involves anything of a legal nature – may have to make threats. A threat is not a deliberately aggressive act, it is a clear statement that, unless a particular course of action is taken, there will be certain consequences: for example, adverse publicity, a formal complaint or legal action. It is unacceptable to threaten any violence or anything illegal. If a threat is made, it will create a reaction, and it is best to make any clear statement about actions to be taken in writing and without emotive language. Making a threat may not fit in easily with the attempts of human service organisations to work in partnership with other organisations. It is also generally considered as inappropriate behaviour in social settings, as well as contrary to much of the professional training on human interaction that the advocate may have had. But a threat may be required to comply with the principles of advocacy. Threats may also have to be carried out, with serious consequences for the other side. The nature of the remedies available to enforce people's rights may ultimately involve the loss of employment for staff of the other side, bad publicity and expense for the other side. This puts the advocate in a strong position, and the inherent power which accompanies it should not be underestimated. It would be unethical for the advocate not to harness such power for the benefit of a client for reasons of inter-agency courtesy.

There is also a distinct tendency for human service professionals who are unfamiliar with the legal or technical aspects of a problem to fall back onto their professional instincts and to try to resolve issues through negotiation as equals with the other side. While a negotiated settlement is best – and is what will be required when dealing with an unbounded problem – even with a bounded problem, a negotiated settlement which produces less than using formal appeal channels is not normally in the client's best interests.

It is important to know the other side's strengths and weaknesses. Most of the welfare bureaucracies that advocates act against have significant weaknesses associated with financial stringency, staff morale, work pressures and public image. All and each of these can be taken into account by the advocate to determine which tactics are likely to be effective in getting the other side to change position.

Another problem with any form of advocacy – especially any which has an undertone of *aggression* – is that it may lead to revenge. This is not a reason for failing to carry out vigorous acts, but one must be aware of it. Any hint of revenge being taken on the advocate or the client must be challenged most vigorously to stop it becoming acceptable.

However, it is a sad fact of life that the other side may treat vigorous advocacy in a personal way and may not be inclined to engage in joint problem-solving on unbounded problems in the future. This can be minimised if it is made clear from the outset that your ethical principles mean that your primary duty when dealing with bounded problems is to act in the client's best interests. This means that different approaches are needed for different scenarios. Having superiors who understand this also helps.

Making a threat is perceived as aggressive behaviour, but it is better to view this as properly channelled aggression in pursuit of a legitimate cause. Failing to channel this aggression into formal threats but resorting to personalised remarks to the other side about their conduct does not advance the cause, whereas a threat to litigate or publicise bad practice will act as a significant lever and may obtain the result that is needed for the client where the problem requires such an approach.

Aggressive behaviour to be avoided includes sarcasm, belittling remarks, deliberate antagonistic behaviour, name-calling and finger-pointing. Recognise your anger, understand how it comes across, its causes, and try to respect the other side's personal integrity. Obtaining a lasting, positive result for a client need not involve humiliating the other side.

How to be assertive in advocacy

There is no simple way to develop the right level of assertiveness in advocacy. However, an awareness of one's own assertiveness and of the common techniques for behaving in an assertive manner will help. There are a number of practical ways in which you can act usefully in the best interests of your client which are compatible with assertive behaviour.

First, as I have discussed, be clear about your objectives and your ethics. You are not in partnership with the other side but you must achieve the best you can, regardless of your personal feelings towards the client. Second, remember that all advocacy must have a structure (see Chapter 11). The lack of a structure will not only make you less efficient as an advocate but will lead to situations where you may act inappropriately. Third, vigorous advocacy on bounded problems must be carried out in a formal manner. This is for tactical, legal and behavioural reasons. It is this third aspect which exemplifies good advocacy practice in such cases.

Behaving formally as an advocate means that you must see the problem not as a personal crusade and not as the other side deliberately discriminating against your client. There are cases when advocates have strong personal views about the injustice of what has been done to a client, and these are important motivating factors. However, these personal views must be recognised and put on one side.

There may also be cases where there is a suggestion that the other side has deliberately discriminated against a particular client. It may be difficult to be precise about when discrimination occurs, and its mere hint can infuriate and affect your judgement. Advocacy must be seen as a clinical activity if objective judgement is to be maintained.

Formal advocacy activity will involve a number of specific techniques:

1   Putting things in writing
2   Viewing individuals' problems as symptoms of a wider malaise
3   Regarding it as positive to complain
4   Considering the role of publicity to change matters
5   Having a good understanding of the facts
6   Having a good understanding of any relevant technical, procedural or legal aspects

Put it in writing

Much of this section will only be relevant when advocating on bounded problems. Something that is said can always be distorted, while something on paper is less easily ignored. When advocating for a client, it can be important to concentrate on the written word. It can seem easier to negotiate on a bounded problem over the phone, but there are distinct disadvantages to advocating verbally: there will be no record of what was said by whom and what was agreed. All advocates can recall situations when the other side agreed to something and then failed to do it, citing the absence of a formal request, or a different interpretation of what was agreed.

Verbal negotiation can also easily lead to the advocate not being sufficiently assertive, or the situation becoming personal if either side becomes heated. Advocates may have to be 'unreasonable' in the eyes of the other side. Tempers may become frayed if negotiations are conducted verbally. For example, an advocate who is acting for a client who has rent arrears with a housing association may be trying to maximise the client's income. The association may phone and ask what they can do to assist. The correct ethical response is to ask the association to withdraw action against the client. The association are unlikely to respond positively to such a suggestion in the circumstances, and such a request needs to be put in writing to keep the heat out of the situation.

Conducting negotiations in writing also means that there is a clear record of events, and this may be important if the matter ever has to be dealt with by a court or tribunal. Thus the letters need to be formal in style.

Written communication is more likely to gain a response. Verbal communication is easily forgotten. Even when face-to-face negotiation occurs on an unbounded problem, some form of written confirmation can be important, and it is a fact of life that something said on headed paper will always be taken more seriously than something said on the phone or handwritten. If there is any chance that the letter may be 'lost', a few pence extra ensures that the letter is sent by Recorded Delivery.

If you send a written communication, you should keep a copy. If it has not been replied to within a specific timescale, send a reminder with a copy. Written negotiation also involves the client. Few clients have typing skills or access to word processors. Your typed letters will look better than anything handwritten, and typing means that copies can be given to the client together with any replies for their comments, so that they are engaged in the advocacy and able to give better instructions. Similarly, you should, generally, write letters dealing with negotiation in such a way that they are in the client's name, and have these signed by the client.

It is possible to build provisos into written communications which are not in the client's name and which include statements of fact. If you are mistaken about facts it makes for difficulties. Unless you are absolutely sure, always precede any statement of fact with the words 'I understand that . . .'. Other difficulties also arise if communications are verbal. Many situations require written requests in order to be effective legally. For example, benefit claims must be in writing, as must requests for reviews of most benefits, to be legally binding. Social services complaints procedures usually require a written request to trigger action, and threats to sue must be in writing making this clear, otherwise the client may be liable for extra costs, etc.

Letters should also contain clear statements of the legal authority for any propositions put forward. Not only does this have more impact but it also makes it clear to the other side that you know what you are talking about. Almost all bounded problems which are subject to advocacy have some legal or procedural issue which can be used to good effect. Legal research skills are thus important, and are explained in Chapter 9.

If the situation is so urgent that the phone must be used, it is still important to confirm the contents of that discussion, and any agreement reached, by letter. There are also one or two situations where the advocate will be putting across complex or subtle arguments. Occasionally it will be more effective to put such matters verbally. Even then the confirmatory letter must still be sent. If the objective is merely to gather facts, then verbal enquiry is effective. But this is information-gathering rather than negotiation or advocacy.

The box below sets out an example of written communication in advocacy on a common bounded problem which exemplifies good assertive practice and incorporates the points made about assertion through writing.

A. Client
5 Anystreet
Anytown
AN7 8NY

National Insurance No.: AB 12 34 56 CD

Date: [today's date]

BY FAX AND POST

Social Fund Section
Department of Social Security
Benefits Agency
Any Road
Anytown
AN1 7NY

Dear Sir or Madam

Please can you review your decision to refuse me a Social Fund grant for a cooker. My existing cooker has stopped working and British Gas advise me that it is dangerous to try to use it. I have two children aged 4 and 2. While they and my partner are generally in good health, absence of hot cooked food can lead to a deterioration in one's health and the alternative of buying take-away foods is not appropriate as it cannot be afforded as we are on Income Support. Therefore, absence of a cooker will also produce exceptional pressure on me and my family because of the additional financial strain. Absence of cooking facilities can also increase the likelihood of children having to be admitted to care.

Consequently, your decision to refuse a grant for a cooker is contrary to Direction 4 of the Secretary of State's Directions on the Social Fund.

This review request must be dealt with urgently. Please contact my representative upon receipt to advise whether or not the refusal will be altered and to arrange a convenient, early date for a formal review interview if the decision is not to be altered. My representative is Ms A D Vocate, Any Department, 2 Anywhere, Anytown, AN2 4NY. Tel. 0123 123456 Ext. 123.

Yours faithfully

A. Client.

Individuals' problems

The problems which advocates often deal with can be symptoms of deep-rooted organisational failure. Such organisational failure thrives on public acceptance of the failure, or public ignorance. Advocates do themselves and their clients no favours by keeping quiet about such issues. If nothing else, they may be storing up more work for themselves by merely responding to individual issues. For example, mistreatment of people in institutions, delays in processing benefit payments, delays in carrying out Community Care assessments, failure by homelessness officials to carry out full, legally binding assessments of housing need, are all classic instances of organisational problems which result in problems for individuals. So . . .

It is positive to complain   An interesting result of the consumerist philosophy affecting welfare provision is that it means that managers are forced to listen more to customers and their representatives. Complaints are thus to be welcomed as an opportunity to improve services, rather than something to be fended off. Going beyond individualism must mean that the advocate not only addresses individual issues but also addresses wider concerns by complaining about the fact that the individual's case may not be a one-off, that the service provided is not acceptable, and demanding that an assurance be given that improvements will be made.

Publicity   Publicising an issue – either by involving the client directly or in less specific terms – is an important part of individual advocacy. Complaining may also raise public awareness of the many imperfections in our welfare system. Obtaining publicity may be particularly difficult for some advocates. However, there is nothing to prevent you advising the client that it would be in their best interests to make their complaint public, and who to contact to do so. Similar considerations apply to involving Members of Parliament or other politicians.

When highlighting issues there are a number of things to be aware of:

1   Journalists like a good story so you will need to highlight controversial aspects of the issue.

2   Journalists can get the wrong end of the stick. This is especially true of complex welfare-orientated issues. Try to ensure that someone briefs the journalist 'off the record' so that errors are less likely. Many journalists also have personal experience of unemployment and family misfortune. This will aid their understanding.

3   A detailed off-the-record briefing may enable you to get away with giving a less contentious quote on the record, but be sure that what you say will be treated in this way.

4   If the client is going on the record about their case, be clear that, if something negative about them comes to light, they or you have a ready answer and they can cope with the ensuing publicity.

5   On-the-record use of a client must always be with their explicit consent. Many will go on the record to help highlight an issue that may be affecting others.

6   Useful results can be obtained by using anonymous case-studies to highlight particular social concerns. The National Association of Citizens' Advice Bureaux have been particularly effective in this respect by compiling reports based upon anonymous case-studies from around the country. Their reports have also covered a wide range of topics.

7   Given the serious social problems that persist in our society, effective change must include altering the causes of these. Publicity is an important aspect of the process of enabling change to happen.

Get your facts right   This applies whether you are publicising an issue or whether you are just concentrating on an individual's case. Good instructions, good interviewing and listening are all part of getting the facts right. If you are not sure of your facts, say so. If the facts turn out to be as you suggest then no harm is done, if not then your position may be strengthened. Loss of future credibility can follow if you are perceived as being unreliable or untruthful. Such facts include evidence in support of care and individual needs, as well as any technical or medical evidence to support an argument on an unbounded problem.

Get the law right   Chapter 9 considers the skills needed for legal research. Don't make statements about people's legal or other rights which cannot be substantiated or supported by reasoned argument. Assertiveness in advocacy means that you must include appropriate references to the law and use arguments that work to the client's best advantage. Indeed, being able to do so has a remarkable confidence-boosting effect on an advocate. If the other side say that something can't happen because of legal or other limitations, ask them to provide the precise facts or precise legal authority for the proposition and, if need be, obtain specialist help.

It should by now be clear that assertiveness is an important and useful aspect of the package of skills needed to be an effective advocate. In advocacy, particularly on bounded problems, assertion may need to be formalised in some way. But there are also other dimensions to negotiating with the other side, and these are dealt with in the next chapter.

References

1 Kahn, A. J. et al. (1972), *Child Advocacy*, New York, NY: Columbia University Press.

7 Negotiation

Negotiation is an important element of advocacy. Negotiation is not concerned with trying to reach a compromise or trying to find the middle ground between two parties. It is concerned with obtaining the best possible result – especially if the problem is unbounded and/or the client has much to lose by actively challenging the other side. In any event, effective negotiation must be carried out within the framework of the principles of advocacy set out in Chapter 2, and it must be carried out assertively. As discussed in Chapter 6, negotiation may also have to be undertaken in a formal manner.

When considering negotiation it is also important to be absolutely confident that the issue in question is one which *should* be negotiated. Further, you cannot negotiate to obtain something which is not legally possible. If the problem concerns the use of discretion, there are legal rules concerning the exercise of discretion by statutory bodies which will form a stronger framework for action than negotiation. Do not procrastinate by negotiating rather than advocating solely because you feel it may be more reasonable. You may not be acting in the client's best interests by doing so, and the task of the advocate is not to please the other side but to get the maximum for the client.

Negotiation is most likely to be useful when there really is no alternative. The types of issues which concern advocates will often be those which can be handled more effectively by challenging the other side, rather than seeking to negotiate. Appeals and complaints procedures are usually free, and allow the advocate considerable scope for getting the best result. Similarly, with debt and housing issues, the client may have a stronger case than may at first appear, and the remedies to resolve matters can be very effective.

Negotiation is useful if there is no structure on which to rely for resolving a problem, if there is no effective sanction that the client can use, if the client is unable to or cannot afford to pursue the matter otherwise, or, very occasionally, if continual litigation has not produced a satisfactory result. It is also needed where it is important to persuade the other side of the correct approach. Advocacy by nurses on health matters will normally be of this nature.

Negotiation is also helpful for negotiating sales and purchases and some debt repayments, though, as discussed earlier, the money advice approach means that objective criteria are applied to most debt issues. Disputes about the assessment of people's care needs and about special educational needs can all be successfully negotiated. Employment issues are interesting. These can be dealt with either through negotiation or through straightforward advocacy. Employment rights can be set down in legislation or legally binding statutes. However, the nature of the master–servant relationship is such that it may be counter-productive to advocate vigorously on an employment matter. Equally, it can be disastrous to negotiate when the employer is clearly acting unlawfully and unreasonably and the client's job prospects are in jeopardy. It is a question of careful judgement which has to take into account matters such as the type of employment and the position of the employee, as well as their instructions.

Should it be negotiated?

There is a saying that 'everything is negotiable'. While that may be true of commercial dealings, it may not be the most appropriate course of action when acting as an advocate. Which of the following situations should be approached by negotiation rather than straightforward advocacy, or a mixture of the two?

1   The local water company have sent a letter to someone on a low income threatening to disconnect their water unless full payment of their bill of £300 is made within seven days.
2   A decision by the DSS to refuse a grant from the Social Fund because there is insufficient money in the local budget.
3   A decision by the local hospital to put someone on a waiting list to see a consultant. The waiting list is 18 months long.
4   A refusal by the council housing department to grant a tenant with rent arrears a housing transfer in order to be nearer relatives who provide care.
5   Suspension of someone's Unemployment Benefit because they lost their last job as a result of misconduct. They are now suffering hardship.
6   Maintenance arrangements for children following a separation.
7   An employee who is given a final warning by their employer for alleged poor work. The employee disputes this.
8   A doctor's decision to treat an elderly woman as a low priority, even though the treatment would mean that her quality of life would be vastly improved.

Suggested answers

1   Rely on an advocacy stance in the first instance as the company may be in breach of their Licence Conditions.

2   Advocacy rather than negotiation. Various formal channels for challenging such a refusal exist. It is also important to raise such a matter with the media, MP and senior civil servants as it will affect many others.

3   Negotiation. Supporting medical evidence is needed. If the law were to provide time limits for waiting lists, this case should not be negotiated. Local performance targets and the Citizens' Charter may provide some leverage for advocacy.

4   Advocacy at first, as there are rules on how transfers should be carried out and how discretion should be exercised. Negotiation if this fails.

5   Advocacy. There are clear legal rules and many ways in which one can challenge such decisions and obtain a good result – even in the most hopeless of cases.

6   Negotiation would be useful, but there is increasingly limited scope for this because of Child Support legislation, so advocacy may have to be used to resolve disputes about maintenance figures set by the Child Support Agency.

7   Negotiation would appear to be appropriate, though it may be necessary to consider an advocacy approach if there are formal appeal procedures and the employee is in a secure position.

8   Negotiation. Creative and assertive arguments in favour of the patient would be needed as 'shortage of resources' may be the initial response.

Negotiation strategy

All negotiation must have a strategy. To negotiate without a clear strategy is to sail into uncharted waters, with all the attendant risks. Neither should negotiation be a matter of either being 'hard' or 'soft' on the other side. An established approach to negotiation strategy divides it into two parts: A, the preparation and B, the actual negotiation. Essentially, it requires the negotiator to be clear about their objectives from the outset and to be well-prepared.

A   Preparation

1   Identify relevant facts
2   Identify any relevant legal issues
3   Conduct legal research
4   Conduct research on any personal and technical aspects that may be relevant and helpful
5   Identify client's goals and interests, and prioritise
6   Identify other side's goals and interests and prioritise
7   Identify strengths and weaknesses of client's position
8   Identify strengths and weaknesses of other party's position
9   Identify possible concessions
10   Consider alternative settlement options
11   Consider alternatives available if negotiation fails

12   Develop agenda
13   Decide upon style (e.g. problem-solving, aggressive, co-operative)
14   Plan tactics (e.g. timing of offers, limited authority, silence, good guy–bad guy, split the difference, threats and promises, take it or leave it, etc.)

B   Negotiation

1   Obtain information through questioning
2   Separate the people from the problem:

    a   listen to the other side
    b   confirm understanding of other side's position
    c   allow other party to let off steam

3   Focus on interests, not positions:

    a   describe problem in terms of impact on client
    b   encourage other side to explain client's interests and goals
    c   explain own client's interests and goals
    d   identify shared interests and goals
    e   focus on present and future concerns, not past grievances

4   Ascertain scope of other party's authority
5   Develop and discuss alternative settlement options
6   Make offers that are justified by objective criteria
7   Insist on and probe for objective criteria based on law, precedents, facts or evidence
8   Be open to reason, closed to threats
9   Make a note of agreements and concessions as they occur[1]

Both during and at the end of any negotiation, it is important to measure the results against some objective criteria in order to assess how effective the negotiation has been: what was conceded by the other side and how far your original objectives were met are useful bottom-line markers for such an exercise.

Negotiation styles need to be thought through deliberately. A competitive negotiation style is characterised by the following:

- Use of threats, intimidation, superiority and blame
- Making extreme demands, making very few or small concessions
- Creating false issues

Such an approach can create misunderstandings between the two sides and make it harder to reach agreement. It raises the likelihood of retaliation and can increase the number of failed negotiations. If used repeatedly, it has been found to be less effective than other styles. However, this approach means that the risk of exploitation by the other side is minimised.

A co-operative style of negotiation is based on:

- Establishing common ground, emphasising shared values
- Making unilateral concessions, seeking highest joint outcome

However, there is strong likelihood of manipulation and exploitation.

A third approach has been described as a principled or problem-solving style.[2] This is characterised by:

- Negotiating on the merits of a case rather than through bargaining
- Focusing on interests rather than positions
- Inventing solutions which will produce a mutual gain for both sides
- Avoiding tricks and posturing
- Insisting that the end result is based on a fair, objective standard
- Separating the people from the problem – don't allow things to become personalised

The aim of such a style is to produce an outcome which meets the needs of your client and, effectively, produces a 'win' without making the other side feel that they are losing. Or, as a Chinese proverb says: 'Build golden bridges for your enemy to retreat over.' This is a mature style which enables you to win while enabling the other side to keep face. It is useful provided, as indicated earlier, negotiation really is the best or only option.

Problems in negotiation

There are a number of problems that can arise during negotiation. Some are sufficiently radical that they will completely undermine the negotiation and produce either a stalemate or a set-back for the client. The problems are not just connected with the conduct of the other side. The most common problems caused by the other side have been described by Fisher and Ury as being of three types:

- The other side being too powerful
- The other side refusing to negotiate meaningfully
- The other side behaving unpleasantly, deceptively or inconsistently[3]

Fisher and Ury suggest a number of responses to each of these scenarios in order to ensure that the negotiator is able to operate from a better position.

The other side is too powerful

It is, of course, assumed that the other side is too powerful. There can be a lot of bluffing and the client may well have a view that the other side is omnipotent. In reality, most of the organisations making up the other side are quite vulnerable, and the client is in a stronger bargaining position than may at first be appreciated. Even though the client's legal rights are weak, there can be considerable organisational impact as a result of tying up senior people from the other side in negotiations or the potential loss of credibility if negotiations fail. Moreover, if the other side won't negotiate effectively, this may trigger a right to use complaints procedures which then put the client and advocate in a stronger position, as it is a return to structured issues and makes the problem into a bounded one.

Fisher and Ury also suggest that if the other side are too powerful, the client and advocate should develop a BATNA – a Best Alternative To a Negotiated Agreement. This should be done at the outset. A BATNA is not a 'bottom line'. Bottom lines tend to be set too low or too high. A BATNA is:

> the standard against which any proposed agreement should be measured. That is the only standard which can protect you both from accepting terms that are too unfavourable and from rejecting terms it would be in your interests to accept . . . your BATNA . . . has the advantage of being flexible enough to permit the exploration of imaginative solutions. Instead of ruling out any solution which does not meet your bottom line, you can compare a proposal with your BATNA to see whether it better satisfies your interests.[4]

A good example of a BATNA involves the sale of a house. Instead of having a bottom-line monetary figure below which offers are not acceptable, the seller must have a series of scenarios in response to offers that are made. There will be a point where the offers may be less than expected but the alternative would be to have an unsold house. Identification of the options thus forms one's BATNA. It is of course also important to try to establish or estimate the other side's BATNA.

The other side refuses to negotiate meaningfully

This can include an outright refusal to negotiate. If this occurs, a common response is to try to be more insistent on negotiating, or to give in and lose. Either is unsatisfactory. Assuming that there are no sanctions you can bring to bear in the situation – negotiation would not be the best option if sanctions *could* be used effectively – the way ahead is to attempt to get the other side to focus on the merits of a solution to the problem.

This may be possible by direct communication and by getting the other side to explain their refusal. Criticism can be deflected by agreeing with it and ensuring that the criticism is seen as symptomatic of the need to address the problem. At this stage, if negotiations have been by phone or letter, a 'without prejudice' meeting can alter the dynamics – and you can gain considerably more influence by taking the initiative in suggesting a meeting to discuss the problem. If even this fails, consider how a third party may be brought in to get negotiations going.

The other side behaves unpleasantly, deceptively or inconsistently

In other words, they resort to dirty tricks. It is important not to personalise the issue, and to get the problem out into the open. This can have a useful cathartic effect. If there is deception, it will be important to recognise this and to ensure that agreements are written and watertight enough to prevent the other side reneging. Similarly, do not respond to any threats made, but do write them down if they are made verbally. Above all, stay cool. When it's all over, you may be able to sort the problem out by taking up the conduct of the other side elsewhere.

There are, of course, many other aspects to negotiation and the skills it requires. As stated earlier, the key issues are:

- Recognition that the problem must be resolved via negotiation rather than advocacy
- Good preparation and strategy
- A clear understanding of different approaches to advocacy and a refusal to let the other side get you down

---

Negotiate it!

This is an exercise in negotiation. Read through the following scenario. Then sketch out a negotiation strategy. Include the following:

- An understanding as to whether or not this is an issue to be negotiated and if so, why
- Likely strengths and weaknesses of both sides' arguments
- The most productive approach for your client
- A BATNA if negotiations fail
- Identification of the *interests* of each party, rather than their *positions*
- Possible solutions which might result in a mutual gain

Mary is a clerk in a medium-sized organisation. You are a friend. Mary started work six weeks ago and has been late for work on 60 per cent of the days since she started. Normal work hours are from 8.45 a.m. until 5.15 p.m., with an hour's lunch break. When she has been late, she has arrived between 20 and 30 minutes late. The times are recorded on a clocking-in machine. In addition, Mary has left

---

work early on four days out of the last five. Her manager has spoken to her about her timekeeping and told her that she has just one chance to improve or her contract will be terminated.

Mary has approached you for help. She tells you that she is a single parent and her childminding arrangements are unreliable. Her mother looks after her 4-year-old son, but she will frequently not turn up to collect him until late, and in the last week her mother was ill so she had to leave him with neighbours. Mary does not earn enough to pay a registered childminder. You also know from your experience as a shop steward that there are formal procedures to be followed for dismissing members of staff, and it is apparent that these have not been followed by the manager.

Mary is anxious to keep this job. Unemployment in the area runs at 20 per cent, this is her first permanent job for five years, and she is very wary of upsetting her new employer. Her manager has a reputation as an unreasonable, duplicitous and vengeful person.

Any negotiation or advocacy will require you to be well-organised and to know how to make the best use of your time and resources, and this subject is dealt with in the next chapter.

References

1   The Continuing Legal Education Society (1989), *Negotiation Outline*, Vancouver.
2   Fisher, R. and Ury, W. (1986), *Getting to Yes – Negotiating Agreement Without Giving In*, London: Hutchinson.
3   Ibid.
4   Ibid.

8 Self-management

Self-management is the skill of making optimum use of yourself as a resource for the client. To be an effective advocate you have to be well-organised and methodical. And, as you will often be working with very limited resources and for clients who are often in desperate situations, self-management is an important way of ensuring the client receives the best service possible. The impact of advocacy is lessened when the advocate has not tackled issues of self-management. Self-management covers a range of activities, and these are as relevant and useful in other areas of your work as they are in advocacy.

Self-management in advocacy will encompass the following:

- Time management
- Report writing
- Creative thinking
- Decision making
- Stress management

Time management

Time management is the skill of making the best use of the time available to you. There are only 24 hours in a day, and you cannot create more. People who work in human service organisations know, only too well, just how much work there is to get through, and the pressure of this can be immense. Learning to make the best use of your time and how to distinguish between pressure from too much work and the type of work will aid survival and make pressures more bearable.

Time management has been the subject of several books, and there is a considerable industry devoted to training us to be more efficient in our work. This has led to some people claiming to be experts in the subject when they are not, and a degree of cynicism about the value of time management.

The first stage is for you to recognise that there will always be room for improvement in how you manage your time. To refuse to accept this is to invite trouble and to deny reality. All of us develop time-wasting habits which can soon eat into the day and, over time, result in much work not being done. The next stage is to do something about it.

Effective use of your time is important in advocacy for a number of reasons:

1   Much of the work which advocates do must be followed up if it is to be effective. For example, letters which the advocate writes to the other side may not be replied to in a timely manner. This is not acceptable, and the advocate must have a system in place for chasing up letters which are not responded to in good time. A tray for copies of letters which need following up is a good idea; computers can be used to generate reminders, and to keep a log of incoming work and outgoing mail.
2   Badly-planned advocacy takes up time. This is then unsatisfying and the advocate loses motivation to do good advocacy in the future.
3   Undertaking advocacy over the phone may appear to be quicker. It often isn't and, as indicated earlier, phone calls must be followed up with a letter. Phone calls can also deteriorate into quasi-social chats.
4   Advocacy is a methodical activity which requires forward planning. Not allowing enough time for this, or for more straightforward preparation, can often result in more time having to be spent resolving the resulting problems, as well as increasing the likelihood of losing the client's case.
5   Advocates are often dealing with regulated systems which have legally binding time limits. Exceeding those limits can have a detrimental effect on the client's situation – for example, time limits for appeals on benefit matters, employment issues and time limits for legal action on homelessness.

Where does all the time go?

A useful exercise is to work out how well you use time. This involves keeping a detailed record of what you do in a typical day. It is a bit laborious to compile such a record but it can show where time is obviously not being well spent. Sometimes the results can surprise even the most organised person. Take a typical day and compile a record of your time using the chart below, which you should photocopy and fill in.

Date ....

Activity	Start	End	Duration	Interruptions by whom (indicate with P if planned or U if unplanned)

The basic rules of effective use of time can be summarised as follows:

1   Handle each piece of paper only once. Some paper can go straight in the bin or be filed away. The important thing is to make a quick decision about what to do with the paper and then, as far as possible, deal with it. Procrastination wastes time and irritates others.

2   Don't talk too much. It can be difficult to time your phone calls in particular, as these can digress, with the consequent loss of valuable time.

3   Don't write too much, and stick to what is relevant. There is an optimum length for every document. Written submissions in support of a client's case must contain the relevant facts, and full enough exposition of the relevant legal and procedural arguments, but do not include facts which don't matter. Apart from the obvious potential for breaches of confidentiality, these can divert the other side's attention from the main issues – for example, is it necessary to include details of someone's childhood traumas when writing on their behalf to get money from the social security system? It is also surprising how much time can be spent on overlong sentences and inclusion of unnecessary phrases.

4   Concentrate and listen. Active listening means that you are better able to judge what is relevant and less likely to miss something which then has to be gone over again in more detail later – with all the implications for time use.

5   Organise your office. A tidy office is more likely to mean that you know where things are, and so are less likely to waste time searching for something when it's needed. Office layouts can also be designed so that less time is wasted by walking about or reaching to get things – a speeded-up video of office activity can be revealing. If an office is shared, less time may be wasted on idle discussions if desks do not face one another.

6   Delegate. Advocates need support as much as anyone else. Good administrative and clerical back-up is essential to ensure that you do not waste time on unnecessary tasks. Delegation also means that you can ...

7   Concentrate on what really matters. Probably 80 per cent of our time is spent less productively than it should be, and only 20 per cent of tasks really make a difference. Identify this 80/20 split in your working day.

8   Meetings matter, so make sure they have a clear purpose, structure and agenda. Set definite times to start and finish, and this will create more time for other things. This applies to all meetings, including any with the other side.

9   Avoid interruptions. Interruptions eat up time – some interruptions can't wait, but most can. Devise a system for filtering out unnecessary interruptions, and organise the incoming flow of work. Having colleagues on a rota is a good way of doing this.

10   Use the diary. Always write appointments down. Use the diary to plan

the time you need to attend to desk-bound tasks – such as lengthy written submissions to the other side and time for follow-up work. Most callers' problems are not urgent, and working by appointment is proven as a more effective way of handling incoming work. Equally, set up systems to deal with emergencies – this may include having to change appointments around to fit in a client. A diary can also be used to keep a . . .

11 'To Do List'. A list of tasks to be done is an essential reminder. You can rank these in order of priority so that the critical 20 per cent are done first.

12 If nothing else, read something about time management and invest some time on a course.

Report writing

Advocates should write frequently. In addition to the style of letter which is sent in the client's name, advocates can find that it is necessary to write longer documents as part of their advocacy. For example, it may be necessary to write a report in support of an application for rehousing, prepare a written submission for a tribunal or other appeal hearing, or a report for a case conference. The style and content will have a significant impact on the other side and the people acting as arbiters. A poorly thought out document or one which is badly presented detracts from your essential message and can weaken an otherwise strong case: hence we will now consider some of the principles of good practice in report writing. The phrase 'report writing' is used because it is a good general description of the task. Strictly speaking, written communications by advocates will not usually be the sort of documents which most people think of as 'reports'.

Before committing pen to paper, consider the following:

1 The purpose of the document.
2 The intended readership.
3 How it should be laid out. Should there be a contents page? Should particular care be taken to have the document word-processed in a particular style? Should it have illustrations, numbered paragraphs, numbered pages, etc?

A written submission in support of a client has distinct advantages. It helps you to state the facts of the case formally, and to reinforce arguments. Having a written record of the arguments has a greater impact than the use of the spoken word alone. Speech can be used to reinforce or expand points in the written submission, so care needs to be taken with written arguments. A golden rule of any presentation – including something in writing – is first to tell the audience what you are going to tell them. A synopsis does this and provides an at-a-glance guide for the intending reader. It immediately helps them focus their thoughts on your message. The facts should be summarised at the beginning, with supporting arguments in a quite separate section. As far as possible, references should be given for all propositions put forward – especially those which are legally based.

The skills of speaking will be relevant in backing up the written arguments. These can be deployed at any time, and they are covered in Chapter 10 in the context of litigation.

Creative thinking and decision making

Advocates will often be faced with situations which appear both intransigent and desperate: any legislation which should protect the client appears to work against them, and the other side seems utterly intractable. While there are rules and techniques of interpreting legislation to the best advantage of the client, there are techniques of creative thinking which can help in this process and which can produce some startling solutions. Creative thinking is also very important in negotiating. For example, it can help the advocate identify possible 'golden bridges' for the other side to retreat over, as well as a BATNA.

The concept of creative thinking starts from the position that we adopt learned responses to problems and learned ways of solving them. When under pressure, our original learned responses will surface. Most learned responses are based on our early experiences, and we will have formed a particular approach based on our experiences – especially those as a child. Creative thinking aims to break the cycle of learned behaviour and to introduce new elements into our analysis of problems. It also tries to harness the latent creativity and originality that humans can bring to situations, enabling them to be reframed and new solutions to old problems to be found.

Many of the problems which advocates deal with will benefit greatly from creative thinking. Similarly, it is important to understand how we can improve decision making. In advocacy, the advocate will be exercising judgements about the best course of action to take. It is easy for our conditioned and deep-seated behaviour to take over and for us to reach the wrong decision. This happens in everyday situations. For example, how many of us have been swayed by clever advertising and bought a product which, had we applied objective criteria, we would never have purchased? Indeed, whole industries appear to have been built on persuading people to make decisions on subjective and impulsive criteria rather than more logical ones.

In advocacy, decisions reached on the wrong criteria may have a detrimental effect on the outcome for a client. Given the type of issues for the client, the consequences are serious. How can the advocate apply creative thinking and better decision making?

The roots lie in advocacy's ethical principles (see Chapter 2). Principle 1 ('Act in the client's best interests'), Principle 4 ('Carry out instructions with diligence and competence') and Principle 5 ('Act impartially and offer frank, independent advice'), all mean that the onus on the advocate of finding the best solution requires creative thinking and objective decision making. Indeed, Principle 5 would appear to imply that any method of making a judgement has to refer to objective criteria rather than the feelings and supposition that characterise much of our day-to-day existence.

When advocates deal with bounded problems set within a regulated framework, creativity has to include imaginative views on the interpretation of words and phrases. There are accepted norms for this which are considered in Chapter 9. However, the process of reaching the best interpretation requires the advocate to consider the problem from several angles. It is also important to think ahead and to try to work out what the other side's view will be and how they will respond. The other side may not be rational in their response – and neither may the legislation nor any other bedrock of the regulated structure. Consider the following example.

Creativity can also involve suspension of judgement. Because our learned

---

Creative puzzle

A council refuse collection service issues new dustbins to all residents. These bins have wheels and are specially designed to be lifted up by equipment on the back of refuse lorries. All the residents have had a letter from the council informing them how the new bins will operate and the advantages of the new scheme. The letter tells residents that they must put their bins 'at the curtilage of your property' and that 'bins that are overflowing will not be emptied as it can damage the machinery on the lorries'.

One resident leaves his bin on his front lawn, as to leave it elsewhere would involve blocking his drive and so be dangerous when driving in or out. The refuse service ignores the bin when on their rounds and do not empty it. The resident then phones the council, who say that the bin must be put at the curtilage. The resident leaves the bin another week, by which time it is overflowing with rubbish. The refuse service don't empty it again. Another phone call to the council elicits the response that the bin could not be emptied as it was too full.

What is the correct approach? Write down a solution for the resident on a piece of paper.

Now consider the following points:

1   Section 45 (1) of the Environmental Protection Act 1990 imposes a duty on local authorities to collect household waste. This Act enables the local authority to insist that householders use certain types of bin for collection and to make conditions about where these should be placed.
2   The word 'curtilage' is defined in a standard dictionary as 'a court or area of land attached to and including a dwelling house'. A legal dictionary has an identical definition. It does not mean 'edge' as the council letter perhaps intended, so their exercise of legal powers in this respect appears not to be justified by the phrasing of their letter.
3   The Local Government Ombudsman is empowered to investigate cases of maladministration. Maladministration was defined in the case of *R* v. *Local Commissioner for Administration for North East England, ex parte Bradford MBC* [1979] 2 AER 881 as including 'bias, neglect, inattention, delay, incompetence, ineptitude, perversity, turpitude, arbitrariness and so on'.
4   In the case of *Dyer* v. *Dorset County Council* [1988] 3 WLR 213 'curtilage' was defined as being 'some small and necessary extension' to a building.
5   Common law principles concerning the law of negligence mean that wrongdoers are responsible for the effects of their negligent actions, but victims must take steps to mitigate their loss. Experience shows that large organisations will usually try to settle a claim against them rather than defend it – especially where the amount claimed is small. Using the wrong wording in a letter could be viewed as negligent, and the resident has incurred a loss.
6   The council's Citizens' Charter states that residents whose bins are not emptied after more than three days will be entitled to £1 compensation for each day of late collection unless the late collection was caused by the resident not following the council's instructions on bin emptying.
7   The council's letter was not approved by the full council, and the power to issue instructions does not appear to have been delegated to the officers. In law, where a council has duties or powers, they must formally agree to delegate these, otherwise anything done by the council's staff in pursuance of these powers and duties is of no force.
8   The resident establishes that a private refuse collection service will empty the dustbin, but they will charge £25 for doing so. The resident just wants to get his overflowing, smelly bin emptied as soon as possible.

This scenario illustrates the importance of establishing:

1   The facts
2   Whether or not the problem is bounded or unbounded, by identifying any legal framework (almost all human activity is governed by rules, so one can often identify a framework)
3   The importance of taking time to identify objective criteria rather than rushing to a conclusion based on assumptions or emotions

behaviour constricts our thinking onto well-worn tramlines, suspending the barriers to thought can be highly productive. We have all experienced conversations with another person where ideas are thrown about and developed to find a solution to a mutual problem. Suspension of judgement accelerates such a process and removes the inhibitions normally present in social situations.

The best-known form of creative thinking is known as 'brainstorming'. Brainstorming is usually undertaken in a group, but there is no particular reason why it should be confined to group situations. Brainstorming can be carried out by an individual – though having another person involved does help. To brainstorm, take a large piece of paper. Write the problem on the top. Then completely suspend judgement and write down the first things that come into your head (or which are spoken out loud by another person), no matter how bizarre or apparently unconnected the words are. The important thing is that this process can throw up some solutions not previously considered. In advocacy, brainstorming can be used to help find a new approach to existing problems, to develop a negotiation strategy, or to help find a new interpretation for words and phrases when the accepted interpretation has been unhelpful.

The process of decision making implies a degree of problem-solving in much the same way that creative thinking does. The process of effective decision making can start much earlier in the advocacy process when the advocate is first interviewing the client and obtaining instructions. Reaching a decision by objective criteria can assist in helping to identify the problem and possible options. A critical aspect of decision making is to establish the criteria for a decision. This involves open discussion about what the outcome should be and the hidden costs of particular courses of action. An example is set out in the box below.

Another creative puzzle

An advice worker is approached by a client with a housing problem. The client has just received a warrant from her private landlord for execution of a Possession Order. This document enables the landlord to evict a tenant, and is effectively the equivalent of 'the eleventh hour'. Not only must a landlord go to court to get possession of a property, but he or she must also go a stage further and obtain the necessary right to carry out (or execute) the order.

The tenant is a single parent on Income Support who ran up £250 arrears of rent during a short spell when she tried working. The complex interaction between various means-tested benefits meant that she missed out on claiming Housing Benefit during this short spell of work, hence the arrears. The Possession Order was taken out because of these rent arrears. The client does not specify a particular need in her instructions, she just wants some 'general advice' on what to do.

Clearly the situation is urgent. Eviction will mean loss of her home and, even though she will qualify for temporary housing from the local council when she is homeless, they may decide that she is 'intentionally homeless' and thus block her route to permanent housing. What are the criteria for reaching a decision about the best action to take?

Likely criteria:

1   The urgency
2   The serious threat to her home
3   The cost of doing or not doing something
4   The personal cost of moving house – e.g. change of schooling
5   The range of remedies

The likely remedies include:

- Applying to the court to have the warrant set aside
- Applying for the possession order to be set aside
- Negotiating with the landlord not to implement the warrant
- Making a backdated claim for any Housing Benefit that should have been paid during the short spell of work
- Applying as homeless to the local council
- Helping the client find somewhere else to live, and helping with the practical arrangements of a move

These criteria should then be put into order of priority. One way to do this is to rank them as either 'Essential' or 'Desirable'. Getting them prioritised means that the advocate is able to judge which remedies should be used. Perhaps all of the remedies could be used, and perhaps the client would even be agreeable to any of them being used singly or in combination. The advocate's ethical principles drive the prioritisation of the criteria, primarily Principle 1, 'Act in the client's best interests'. Helping the client find somewhere else to live may make the advocate feel good. It is unlikely to eliminate the debt, will create additional expense, and doesn't save the client's home. Negotiating with the landlord may be effective, but relies on the landlord conceding a point. It also means that there is still a warrant hanging over the client. The effect of Principle 1 when used to prioritise the criteria is that the more legalistic remedies are explored. Even if the advocate is unfamiliar with these, the criteria should lead to a better conclusion than otherwise, and the advocate should make an informed referral to someone who *is* familiar with such remedies.

This puzzle shows the value of using some form of criteria to reach a decision and to bring about a degree of objectivity that would be lacking had the advocate just acted in accordance with past experience and knowledge.

Stress management

The aim of this section is to introduce the reader to some basic concepts associated with stress management. There are a number of publications available which go into much more detail, but it is important that stress management is seen as one of the skills associated with effective advocacy.

Advocacy is stressful. It is stressful because the advocate may feel over-awed by the other side, by a lack of confidence or by a lack of knowledge. Advocacy also induces stress because the client will often be stressed, and this is transmitted to the advocate. Above all, the other side's routine actions and attitudes may be completely at odds with the advocate's own deeply-felt values and principles, and may arouse strong feelings in the advocate as a result. This can be stress-inducing. Stress will also be induced by the sheer level of demand upon the advocate and the need to constantly balance competing priorities.

Stress is harmful. Not only is it bad for your health but its effects can lead to you mistiming or misjudging a situation. It can also produce work which is not sufficiently well-prepared and which is not well-presented. In the longer term, stress may lead to burn-out and a loss of motivation. In some cases, this may even necessitate a change of direction in the advocate's career, with the consequent loss of their skills for the benefit of clients. More commonly, stress produces impaired thinking, which in turn leads to poor decision making. This in turn produces worry, and thence more stress.

Conversely, some stress is often required to keep the advocate working at an optimum level, to stimulate creativity and competent, fast responses – in effect, to prevent 'rust-out'. Controlled stress can be good for you, but there must be recognition of the optimum level of stress for each individual. This means that the advocate in a human service organisation must recognise and learn to manage stress if it is to be used for the benefit of the client.

As with most things, the beginning of a solution starts with recognition of the problem, or, in some cases, recognition that there *is* a problem. Individuals' reactions to stress often appear quite logical; in reality, stress has a blinding effect and creates an illusion which is ultimately counter-productive.

Different personality types react to stress in different ways. Four main personality types have been characterised as having differing reactions to stress:

- Type 1 personalities are non-assertive and have difficulty in recognising when stress is a problem.
- Type 2 personalities are inflexible and find it difficult to adapt to change.

- Type 3 are stimulus-seekers and nothing remains static. Such person-alities have been described as 'stress carriers', as their behaviour and methods of work can increase stress among other people.
- Type 4 personalities are competitive, over-assertive, and have a need to be in control. Their reactions to stress can be aggressive.

While these personality type descriptions are rather crude and, in reality, most people are a mixture of various different personality types, they do provide a rough guide to understanding how we react to stress.

The next stage in managing stress is to recognise the symptoms.

Symptoms of stress

Physiological

- Eye strain or sore eyes
- Difficulty sleeping
- Stomach pains or digestive problems
- Nausea or giddiness
- Headaches
- Increased heartbeat

Emotional

- Irritability
- Anxiety
- Procrastination
- Feelings of failure
- Feeling of an inability to cope
- Irrational dread of future events
- Poor concentration
- Daydreaming

Coping with and reducing stress

It may not always be possible to remove the source of stress, but it may be possible to limit the cause, and it is possible to learn ways of coping with stress, thus making it less of a problem. Identification of the sources of stress is the first step in stress management. It may result from particular types of situation, or it may be a result of lack of effective support for the advocate's work – a particular problem as line managers of advocates in human service organisations often have little face-to-face contact with clients, and may have little understanding of the principles and practice of advocacy.

Positive methods of coping with stress can include:

- Taking regular breaks during work
- Taking proper holidays and using up all of your holiday entitlement
- Assertive behaviour
- Understanding yourself and your emotions
- Developing hobbies
- Relaxation techniques

Negative methods of coping with stress include:

- Overeating
- Drinking
- Emotional outbursts
- Blaming others
- Denying the problem

These should be avoided.

As stated earlier, this section of this chapter did not aim to cover stress management comprehensively. Rather it served to raise the issue and to introduce some basic concepts associated with stress management to help the advocate become more effective.

The next two chapters are primarily concerned with advocacy on bounded problems.

9 Legal research

This chapter is an introduction to the legal concepts involved in advocacy. While some advocacy can be performed successfully using good negotiation skills, without relying on the law or other rules, it is important to establish whether there is a legal basis to a case before commencing negotiations or any other active advocacy. Legal research may also require skilled, appropriate legal help. Despite this, there are many instances where the client does *not* have access to skilled, appropriate legal help, and also situations where advocates in human service organisations can readily undertake the necessary legal research in support of a client.

'Legal research' is a generic term for the skills involved in assembling a coherent and logical argument in support of the client's case. Of course, the basis for your argument may not just be references to the relevant law, but may also include policy and practice statements that the other side has published and which are not being fully complied with. These can be especially relevant in advocacy on care issues or Citizen Advocacy. Similarly, research may be needed on medical and social aspects of a case.

It is particularly important to establish the legal basis of a problem. Almost all areas of human activity are governed by some rule or other, and welfare providers are often subject to very detailed rules, as well as general principles of administrative law which can form a separate line of challenge for the advocate. Legal research also helps sort out the disorganised jumble of facts that may have been presented to the advocate by the client or the other side. It is not unknown for advocates to be bombarded with a mass of irrelevant data. Attention to these irrelevant matters diverts from the key issues and creates confusion. It may also overwhelm the advocate.

Similarly, facts may be uncertain. One side's perception of the facts may be very different to the other's. Again, legal research should enable the advocate to establish the most likely version of facts using techniques which are more reliable than opinions or prejudices about a client or the other side.

Legal research also links directly with the ethical duty of the advocate to 'Act in the client's best interests'. Much legal research is concerned with finding the most effective argument, developing and strengthening the arguments in the client's favour, and finding the best possible and sustainable interpretation of the law.

As well as a jumble of facts to unravel, the advocate may find that more simple problems require research. These can be described as *focused* or *linear problems*. In such cases, the facts will not be in dispute and it is a simple case of pointing out to the other side where they have slipped up. Much advocacy by human service professionals will be of this nature, and it arises because of the appallingly high error rate of welfare bureaucracies.

For example, the Department of Social Security's own Chief Adjudication Officer has consistently indicated that between 50 and 60 per cent of all decisions about Income Support are defective in some way.[1] Housing officials dealing with homeless people often display a staggering lack of knowledge of the law about homelessness, as witnessed by the large number of cases which have ended up in the courts because basic legal issues have been ignored. Similarly, social workers and their managers can be sadly misinformed about the legal obligations inherent in their work. For example, the scathing remarks made by the Local Government Ombudsman in 1992 about Essex Social Services' administration of home care charges.[2]

Another characteristic of focused or linear problems is that they will not require an interpretation. The answer will be clear and unambiguous. Linear problems will also have a legal basis which is not qualified in any way, nor subject to other matters. While linear problems are common, the more complex *curvilinear problems* require enhanced legal research skills, which may also be required in borderline cases. And it is the borderline situations which often appear most unjust and absurd and which, if resolved, will push back the boundaries of accepted practice for the benefit of more clients.

Linear problems

Describing something as being 'linear' means that it has the properties associated with a straight line. There are no curves or bumps to be negotiated. Examples of linear problems which advocates in human service organisations may come across include:

- The minimum age for receiving Attendance Allowance is 65.
- A Community Care Assessment must have a named assessor.
- NHS hospitals must reimburse travel costs for patients on Income Support or Family Credit.
- Children whose parent(s) receive(s) Income Support are entitled to free school meals.
- Benefit for people in hospital is reduced after six weeks.
- Every loan agreement must include details of the Annual Percentage Rate (APR) of interest charged on the loan.

In contrast, consider some examples of what might be described as *moulded curvilinear problems*.

Moulded and unmoulded curvilinear problems

Moulded curvilinear problems are those where the facts are clear and are not in dispute. *Unmoulded* curvilinear problems are those where there is ambiguity and the facts are unclear. Clarification of the facts can make the latter into either moulded curvilinear problems or linear problems. Both types of curvilinear problem require legal interpretation and creative thought to get the best result for the client. For example:

- A claim for most benefits can be backdated if the claimant has 'good cause' for not claiming sooner.
- Certain 16- and 17-year-olds without funds can receive Income Support to 'prevent severe hardship'. This may be interpreted to include those living with families who have insufficient funds to support them.
- Benefit claims must be determined within 14 days unless it is not 'practicable' to do so.
- People who are vulnerable because of 'other special reasons' should be considered as being in priority need under the homelessness legislation, and so have a right to housing.

Dealing with unmoulded problems is most complex of all. Not only will the legal issues be unclear but the facts will be unsorted. In such situations, the advocate's first task is to identify the relevant facts. While good interviewing skills are an essential part of this process, it may also be necessary to get the other side's version of events, to locate important documents, and research into the relevant legal issues may be necessary to clarify which facts need to be determined. Therefore, a preliminary step in legal research is to locate relevant legal and other sources.

This legal activity can become time-consuming and complex. Indeed, for many advocates, the realm of curvilinear problems will be impracticable. However, there are specialists who may be consulted, and often verbal advice from them is all that is needed to resolve the matter.

What is a legal source?

The term 'legal source' is another way of describing a rule. It may be contained in statute form (also called 'primary legislation' or, more commonly, 'Acts of Parliament'), a statutory instrument (also known as 'secondary' or 'delegated legislation' or 'regulation'), or in caselaw. It may also be found in policy and procedures laid down by the other side, but it is far from unknown for these to be contrary to the law, and reliance should only be laid on them if the legal source or authority is unhelpful or too ambiguous. Use of policy and procedures may be helpful to challenge problems such as poor care standards or response times to enquiries where no clear legal guidelines exist. The case-study 'Healthcare – meals for Michael' (see Chapter 3, pages 52–5) demonstrates the use of advocacy where no clear legal guidelines exist.

A frequent problem faced by advocates is a refusal or an insistence by the other side about how something should be done. Often this can lead to staff carrying out procedures which are against the law but which they have difficulty accepting as unlawful because the particular practice has become enshrined in their culture. In my experience this problem is most marked among local authorities, who develop informal ways of ignoring the law. A good example is the flagrant breach of the law requiring local authorities to process housing benefit claims within 14 days. All manner of excuses – from overwork to problems with the rent officer or the computer – can be offered as reasons for not complying with the legal duty to process the claim within this period. A 'we don't bother with irksome details like law here' attitude can prevail.

Faced with a frustrating and unacceptable situation such as this, the advocate may find it helpful to ask the other side to cite the legal authority for their actions – not so that the other side undertakes legal research for the advocate, but so that they gain some insight into the unlawful nature of their acts. It may also be necessary to pursue the constructive use of aggression described in Chapter 6, and indeed to litigate the matter (see Chapter 10), so the relevant legal source must be established before the advocate enters into any negotiations or active advocacy with the other side.

Legal research involves the use of reference works. For an advocate this is the starting and, often, the end point. Fortunately, over the years, excellent reference books on the main areas of activity by advocates have been published and improved (see opposite). The books are competitively priced and regularly updated. Investment in books is a small price to pay given the potential return, and the loss that may occur through under-investment. Even on a practical level, failure to purchase up-to-date reference books can be counter-productive, as an organisation's staff will often be faced with problems that require access to current rights information. The cost of the extra phone calls made to try to establish the information soon outstrips the cost of books.

Basic reference books

Benefits

The *National Welfare Benefits Handbook* and the *Rights Guide to Non-Means-Tested Benefits*, published each April by the Child Poverty Action Group (CPAG). Despite their rather cumbersome titles, these two handbooks comprehensively describe the benefits system. There are also countless footnotes to refer the reader to the exact legal source. Two annual companion volumes, *The Child Support Handbook* and *The Ethnic Minorities Benefits Handbook*, cover related areas. These do become rather detailed for most advocacy, but it is important to obtain them if these issues arise regularly in your work.

The yearly *Disability Rights Handbook* from the Disability Alliance complements the CPAG books. It has a strong emphasis on tactics, and covers a range of areas in addition to disability, so it is also useful for those who do not work with people with disabilities. It contains brief sections on debt, community care, health matters and housing, as well as the main text on benefits issues.

A *Guide to Housing Benefit and Council Tax Benefit* published by Shelter Housing Advice Centre is a more thorough treatment of Housing and Council Tax Benefit than the CPAG handbooks, which will suffice for the vast majority of human service professionals.

More detailed books

The following annual volumes contain annotated extracts from social security legislation. They are perhaps not for the average person engaged in day-to-day advocacy, but I mention them for information purposes, and because they may be available for consultation at good libraries.

- *CPAG's Income-Related Benefits: The Legislation*, by J. Mesher.
- *Non-Means-Tested Benefits: The Legislation,* by D. Bonner, I. Hooker and R. White.
- *CPAG's Housing Benefit and Council Tax Benefit Legislation*, by L. Findlay and M. Ward.
- *Medical and Disability Appeal Tribunals: The Legislation*, by M. Rowland.

Housing

The Housing Rights Guide (1992), by G. Randall, is a straightforward introductory book for those unfamiliar with housing law.

The Manual of Housing Law (1993), by A. Arden and C. Hunter, is an effective presentation which is comprehensive enough to point the adviser in the right direction in most cases.

The Homelessness Code of Guidance (1989), published by HMSO. Housing authorities must 'have regard to' this code, and it contains useful insights into the law, as well as some clear explanations of how duties should be performed.

Homeless Persons (1994), by C. Hunter and S. McGrath. This is an excellent and detailed summary of the law, as well as a guide to mounting legal challenges to refusals of housing.

Debt and Housing Emergency Procedures (1993), by D. Forbes and N. Madge, is a handbook from the Legal Action Group (LAG), designed for use by experts, but worth dipping into by the less expert. It contains interesting and creative arguments on the relevant law. *Defending Possession Proceedings* (1993), by J. Luba, N. Madge and D. McConnell, is a companion LAG volume. It covers both tenants and owner-occupiers who are facing loss of their home.

Debt

A Guide to Money Advice in Scotland (1992), by J. Gray, another book from the CPAG, provides comprehensive guidance on protecting the debtor in Scotland. Those south of the border will need to read the *Debt Advice Handbook* (1993), by M. Wolfe and J. Ivison, also published by CPAG, with many useful standard letters for use when trying to get the best deal for the debtor. The *Debt Advice Handbook* also contains useful summaries about the ethics and skills needed for effective debt advice.

The Rights Guide for Home Owners, by J. McKenny and L. Thompson, published annually by the CPAG. Less detailed than some of the other books on debt, this covers the legal rights of the home-owner, and advises on buying a home and keeping it.

The Fuel Rights Handbook, by A. Hoffland and N. Nicol, contains advice on helping debtors who are in trouble with their fuel bills (usually published annually).

In addition, a series of guides on various aspects of debt are published by the National Money Advice Project, Birmingham Settlement, 318 Summer Lane, Birmingham, B19 3RL.

Social services and health

Very little has been published in this area. This may change as advocacy develops around community care issues. The *Disability Rights Handbook* has much useful information, as does the *Legal Rights Manual* (1994) by J. Cooper. Otherwise, it's a question of getting hold of a more comprehensive work, such as Butterworth's *The Encyclopaedia of Social Services Law.*

Basic reference works will suffice for almost all linear problems and for many moulded curvilinear problems. However, even in those cases, it can be important to refer to the original legal texts.

Finding the law

Legal research will necessitate locating the original sources, and these can be found in any good reference library. Such a library will have law reports containing judgments that make up caselaw, and volumes of statutes and statutory instruments. Procedural and policy documents may have to be obtained from the other side.

Statutes are usually locatable by their title. They can be found in good libraries in volumes bound year-by-year. Another place to locate a statute is in *Halsbury's Statutes*. The advantage of *Halsbury's* is that it is updated annually, and it has a commentary on the legislation. Several of the books cited in the box above also contain extracts from the legislation which are updated regularly in new editions.

A considerable amount of relevant law on welfare issues is found in statutory instruments. These contain the detail of the law in many cases, and they are passed by Parliament using a quicker procedure than statutes. This also means that they are used for the minutiae of the law that are likely to be changed frequently. Use of the most up-to-date, amended version of the statutory instrument is thus particularly important. Statutory instruments are available in HMSO-bound volumes, but there is a risk, especially with those which are more than a year or two old, that they may contain parts of the instrument which are out of date. And, as there are about 14 000 statutory instruments in force, growing at the rate of 3 000 a year, with frequent additions and changes, the risk of referring to dated law is thus quite considerable.

Statutory instruments encompass a vast number of important issues for advocates. The areas currently covered by statutory instruments include:

- Charges for people in residential and nursing homes
- Placement of children with foster parents
- The rules of entitlement to almost all social security benefits
- Rules on access to social services and housing records
- Details of the services general practitioners in the National Health Service are obliged to provide to their patients
- Details of rules for prisoners and prison staff
- Rules governing home improvement and similar grants
- Rules on student grant entitlement
- Child Support Agency maintenance calculation rules

Those reference books or encyclopaedias of areas of the law which contain statutory instruments should be used in preference to other texts. If you are really stuck, the reference library should have copies of works such as *Halsbury's Statutory Instruments*. There is also the useful multi-volume general reference work, *Halsbury's Laws*, which is a good place to start when researching an unfamiliar subject, and will refer you to statutes and statutory instruments, as well as relevant caselaw.

Having located a relevant statute or statutory instrument, remember how they are divided up. Statutes will often have parts and will always have sections, sub-sections and paragraphs. The section will be a bold number on the left margin, and a sub-section will the next number in brackets. Letters below will be paragraphs. A capital letter after a section, sub-section or paragraph indicates that it has been inserted by an amending Act. Thus, S. 5(2) (a) (i) of an Act means section 5, sub-section 2, paragraph (a) (i). To demonstrate, look at the following short extract from the Social Security Contributions and Benefits Act 1992:

> **28.**—(1) Subject to section 29 below a person shall be disqualified for receiving unemployment benefit for such period not exceeding 26 weeks as may be determined in accordance with Part II of the Administration Act if—
>
> (a) he has lost his employment as an employed earner through his misconduct, or has voluntarily left such employment without just cause . . .

I will return to section 28 in a later exercise, as its phrasing is a classic example of curvilinear problems which are capable of considerable flexibility in their interpretation.

Find it – Exercise 1

Find the precise legal authority in a statute or statutory instrument for the following propositions. It would be best to have access to the relevant legislation in order to complete this exercise, and you should begin by using a relevant reference book to find a note which indicates the legislation.

1 A person is homeless if they will lose their accommodation within 28 days.
2 Education Maintenance Allowances should be awarded to pupils aged 16–19 on a low income to help them remain in education.
3 Extra Housing Benefit can be awarded to someone in receipt of Housing Benefit if they have exceptional circumstances.
4 General practitioners must provide their patients with free certificates for use in connection with benefit claims.

The other important legal source is caselaw. In the Commonwealth's legal systems, caselaw plays a very significant role. First, the higher courts' decisions are binding precedents. Second, large areas of law are based on caselaw rather than legislation. In the welfare law field, caselaw has tended to interpret and guide the law rather than form it, but it is, none the less, important.

In the case of social security law, there is a considerable body of caselaw. Most of these are decisions of the Social Security Commissioners – the appeal body above the locally-based Social Security Appeal Tribunals and similar tribunals. Caselaw will be referred to in annotated reference books, as well as in some of the more general works.

The most confusing aspect of caselaw is also the easiest. This is the system of letters and numbers used after the title of a case – the case reference. The case reference enables the researcher to find the full report of the judgment of the case. It is within the judgment that the actual precedent will be found. Precedent is rarely a matter of applying the same solutions to the same facts. It is more often concerned with general principles – when a similar point arises in another case, the ruling on that point must be followed in accordance with the principles laid down in the earlier case, unless there is a distinction. The application of these principles renders caselaw a source of legal authority.

Fortunately, almost all significant cases are reported. The reporting of cases is undertaken by a variety of private firms and by the courts themselves. Commissioners' decisions are reported by HMSO, but there are also unreported decisions which are simply a copy of the decision of the commissioner. Each reported court case will have a case reference so that it can be located in the volumes of law reports (again, these can be found in good reference libraries). Cases will also be referred to in reference books, or in notes in annotated books on legislation, using the case reference. Here are some examples:

- *Hill* v. *Harris* [1965] 2 AER 358
- *R* v. *Secretary of State for Social Services, ex parte CPAG and others* [1989] 3 WLR 1116.
- *R* v. *Gough* [1993] AC 646

The first case is a case on the law of contract which is a dispute between two private parties. The square brackets are a convention used for certain types of reported case. The letters AER stand for All England Reports, a series of commonly available law reports. Most published law reports use square brackets, and they will contain the year in which the case was reported. The use of square brackets is not significant, and is merely a convention. The number before 'AER' gives the volume number, and the last number is the page number of that year's volume where the case can be found.

The second case is the law report of a judicial review case. These have a distinctive description in a case reference as, technically speaking, the Crown *(R)* is being used to take action to control a body. Judicial review is the most significant legal sanction for advocates in human service organisations. I will discuss its use in Chapter 10. The case reference for this case uses the same conventions as the All England Reports, but this time the reports are the Weekly Law Reports, another published series.

Finally, the last case is a criminal case: the Crown acting against Gough. AC refers to an Appeal Court. There are many published law reports, all of which use a distinctive format. A law dictionary will carry a list of the abbreviations and their meaning.

Decisions of Social Security Commissioners use a different form of case reference, for example: R (U) 24/87. This stands for the twenty-fourth reported decision on Unemployment Benefit in 1987. Other letters are used to describe other benefits. Unreported decisions have a different case reference. For example, CU 89/1987. This means the eighty-ninth case on Unemployment Benefit submitted to the commissioner in 1987. If an unreported decision becomes reported, the numbering is altered to fit in with the reported system.

Finding a case reference is often not hard. Finding the relevant law reports will be harder, as you will need to obtain access to the original documents. Most reference books will explain the point of law expounded in the law report, which is very helpful, but it can be useful to have access to the actual wording used by the judges in the decision in order to cite them in support of one's own arguments. Having located the report, one should refer to the headnote at the front. This will summarise the relevant facts and the reasons for the decision. Many headnotes will indicate which paragraphs contain the significant reasoning. It is this reasoning which will explain how, for example, words in legislation are to be interpreted, or how a particular course of action should be taken. A more thorough approach is to read through the whole law report.

Find it – Exercise 2

Using standard reference books, find the cases which support the following propositions:

1   The disqualification from receiving Unemployment Benefit should not always be for the maximum 26-week period.
2   Someone should be regarded as 'vulnerable' under the homelessness legislation if they are less able to fend for themselves.

It is often also useful to obtain copies of the other side's internal guidance, procedures or policy. Some of these are easily obtainable, others less so. Local authorities are required to make available to the public most items submitted to council committees. Certain important policy documents must be readily available to the public – for example, policies on allocation and transfer of housing. So must copies of the Community Care Plan and Children's Services Plan, many education policy statements and, in the National Health Service, Standards of Care Statements can be obtained. The Department of Social Security publish a multi-volume *Adjudication Officers' Guide*, and copies of statements about customer service standards and complaints procedures should also be readily available. But the most interesting internal documents may have to be obtained by stealth. As stated earlier, such documents may be useful when the law appears to be unhelpful or non-existent in the problem area in question. In the case of an unbounded problem, the use of policy and procedure documents may help make the problem tangible and bounded, thus making the forthrightness of the advocacy approach more appropriate rather than the more subtle approach of negotiation.

The meaning of words

Ultimately, all rules are about words and what they mean. And it has been stated by a former Lord Chancellor that 'over nine out of ten cases heard on appeal before the Court of Appeal or the House of Lords, either turn upon or involve the meaning of words contained in enactments of primary or secondary legislation.'[3] Often the words in the rules will be clear. At other times the legislation or policy will point you in various directions to other words and phrases. It is important to understand the skills involved in interpreting words and phrases as it enables the advocate to have a significant cutting edge, especially as much welfare law legislation is drafted in haste or without full awareness of the consequences, and policy and procedures may have been drafted with little, if any, thought being given to interpretation.

There are a series of standard steps to be followed when trying to find the meaning of words and phrases. Again, underpinning this process is the ethical duty towards the client and the need to develop the best argument in support of their case. It can be the case that one week it is best to argue that a donkey is a horse and the next week to argue that the donkey is a mule!

One must start by remembering that at first, words can seem to have a clear meaning but they may actually mean something entirely different. The use of the phrase 'severe disability' in various pieces of social security legislation is a good example. The phrase doesn't actually mean 'severe disability' in the commonly accepted sense, but it is defined by reference to a series of regulations that mean only a very small proportion of severely disabled people who happen to receive particular benefits and to live in particular circumstances are 'severely disabled' for the purposes of the legislation.

Therefore words may have a definition inside the legislation itself. Many Acts will have a section devoted to definition of various words and phrases used. In the case of statutory instruments, Regulation 2 of almost all statutory instruments will contain a glossary of definitions of words and phrases used in the legislation, but meanings can be attached to words elsewhere in legislation, or can be inferred from their use elsewhere in the legislation. Even where a glossary is used, there may still be ambiguity about the meaning of words and phrases, or the glossary's definition may itself be ambiguous!

Another means of checking the meaning of words in legislation is to acquire a copy of the Interpretation Act 1978. This will explain, for example, that a reference to 'he' in legislation is also a reference to 'she' unless otherwise specifically excluded.

In other cases, one can refer to another piece of legislation which might contain a useful definition of a word – for example, a case in Australian insurance law was used to define a word in English and Scots social security law – but one can equally argue that such an interpretation should not apply as the legislation was for a different purpose, or that the words have a different meaning when seen in another context. Use of a reference book such as *Stroud's Judicial Dictionary*[4] or *Words and Phrases Legally Defined*[5] will enable you to locate the cases where particular words or phrases have been defined in reported cases.

There are also a number of principles to be followed when interpreting legislation. These are:

1   An Act must be looked at as a whole; words are to be given their meaning as popularly understood at the time of enactment; an Act is presumed not to alter existing law beyond that necessarily required by the Act, etc.
2   Words should be given their ordinary, everyday meaning (the 'literal rule'). A dictionary should be consulted for this.
3   If there is ambiguity, the words should be seen in context and the meaning taken from the words before and after the particular word.
4   If ambiguity still exists, the 'mischief rule' should be applied. This rule is meant to identify the mischief that the legislation was designed to address; or, what was Parliament's intention in passing a particular piece of legislation? In the past it was not acceptable to refer to the statements of ministers in Parliament to establish the intention behind the legislation. It is now acceptable to use reports in *Hansard* as an aid to discovering the mischief and hence the right interpretation of a word.

When considering the words used in policy or procedure documents, these four principles will be equally useful in reaching an interpretation which best supports the client's case. Use of the 'literal rule' and simply looking in a dictionary may often produce the required result, or enable you to point out that the wrong word has been used in a policy or procedure document. You may also find it helpful to consult a standard text on interpretation, such as Maxwell's *Interpretation of Statutes*.[6]

Interpretation in action

The extract from section 28 of the Social Security Contributions and Benefits Act 1992 cited earlier is a useful example of ambiguity in welfare legislation. It is also useful to master, as figures show that only 2 per cent of those disqualified actually appeal but, of them, over 50 per cent are successful. Here is the extract again:

28.—(1) Subject to section 29 below a person shall be disqualified for receiving unemployment benefit for such period not exceeding 26 weeks as may be determined in accordance with Part II of the Administration Act if—

(a) he has lost his employment as an employed earner through his misconduct, or has voluntarily left such employment without just cause . . .

The first point to note is that we are advised that this section is 'subject to section 29 below'. Section 29 states that no disqualification can apply where a person refuses to accept a job in particular circumstances. So it is clear that section 29 refers to other parts of section 28, not the extract we are concerned with.

Returning to the extract from section 28, it appears that someone who has lost employment as an employed earner can, in certain circumstances, be disqualified. What is an 'employed earner'? This phrase is defined in section 2(1) of the Act as 'a person who is gainfully employed in Great Britain either under a contract of service, or in an office (including elective office) with emoluments chargeable to income tax under Schedule E'. So section 28 would not appear to apply to people commonly described as self-employed, nor to those who lose their jobs abroad and who return home and claim benefit. It would also not apply to active volunteers whose service is terminated. But what about councillors? They might appear to be included, as would company directors who are also elected. A person who was employed (but not 'gainfully') who lost their job would also seem not to be caught by the sanctions of section 28. The phrase 'employed earner' appears elsewhere in legislation, and further research could cast more light on its meaning.

Section 28 starts by stating that the period of disqualification is to be for 'such period not exceeding 26 weeks'. Does this mean *all* disqualifications must be for 26 weeks, or are other periods of disqualification possible? The context of this phrase appears to imply that other periods are allowable even though the section clearly states that a disqualification 'shall' be imposed in certain circumstances. Further research in a reference book shows that in R (U) 4/87 it was held that other periods of disqualification are quite possible.

The next words to consider are 'lost his employment . . . through his misconduct . . . ' So the disqualification applies to those who lose their job as a result of misconduct. What is 'misconduct'? A dictionary defines this as 'bad conduct'. Research indicates that further commissioners' decisions exist on this point, and that the word 'misconduct' has been given a common-sense meaning which should be applied with regard to the circumstances of each case: 'conduct which is causally but not necessarily directly connected with the employment, and having regard to the relationship of employer and employee and the rights and duties of both, can fairly be described as blameworthy, reprehensible and wrong'.[7] Even more research would show how this has been applied in practice.

If the employee has not lost the job through misconduct, they must have 'voluntarily left such employment without just cause' – simply leaving voluntarily is not enough. To escape the sanction, the employee must have: a) left voluntarily, and b) without just cause. Clearly there will be situations where a person does leave a job of their own volition but *not* voluntarily. The employer may have made their life such a misery that leaving was the best option. No caselaw seems to exist on this point so we can safely give the word 'voluntarily' its ordinary, everyday meaning. What about the phrase 'just cause'? It is hardly surprising that this is ambiguous given that it is not in common everyday use. Research indicates that no hard and fast rule has been laid down in caselaw. But many cases have been reported which show that a variety of situations – domestic and personal circumstances, a trial period in an unsuitable job, early retirement where the alternative is redundancy, leaving with the firm offer of an alternative job which then fails to materialise, severe grievances about work – have all been held to be 'just cause'. So there is considerable scope for creative argument on behalf of the client who leaves voluntarily.

This demonstration of interpretation shows the scope for creativity in a relatively difficult area where there is substantial caselaw. It is perhaps untypical of the interpretation problems faced by many advocates in human service organisations, but it usefully illustrates the principles of interpretation.

Unravelling facts and reaching conclusions

While factual analysis would appear to be something which is undertaken before looking at the legal sources in support of the client's case, sometimes only legal research can reveal which facts are relevant and which are not. There is a technique for reaching certain conclusions about facts which enables a compromise between the need to reach a balanced conclusion where facts are unclear or disputed, and the ethical duty to act in accordance with the client's wishes and instructions.

As I mentioned in Chapter 6, when asserting facts during contact with the other side, unless the advocate is very sure of the facts, it is best to communicate them in terms of 'I understand that . . . I am advised that . . . ' etc. The advocate can also try to reach a preliminary understanding of the facts by applying a fact-finding technique. The first step is to carry out legal research which identifies the additional facts which may be needed. For example, when advising a client whose Unemployment Benefit has been stopped under section 28 of the Social Security Contributions and Benefits Act, applying principles of interpretation and considering caselaw will necessitate further exploration of facts: 'Why did you leave your last job? Can you describe the pressures of your domestic situation and the poor relationship with your boss that made you give up the job?'

The next step is to write a chronology of the facts and events. This can be a useful aid to clear thinking and when putting the case over to the other side or to an arbitrator. A written chronology is far superior to anything which is committed to the advocate's memory and recounted orally. Obviously, the facts to be included in the chronology are those which are relevant to the issue in question. It is also important to gather documentary evidence in support of any facts, preferably the original documents. Often the other side will have documents relating to the client's case which they are prepared to release. In some cases of non-disclosure, it is possible to take court action to have documents 'discovered'. This forces the other side to release relevant papers, but it will necessitate the involvement of a lawyer to act for the client.

One then goes on to make some preliminary findings of fact – but if your client is clear about their version of the facts, you are ethically obliged to assert those. A finding of fact is based upon the balance of probability and, generally speaking, only those facts which are clearly inherently improbable should be discounted. Do also remember that even the most absurd and unbelievable facts can turn out to be correct.

Fact-finding is a process which runs throughout advocacy, and which requires good interviewing skills as well as a good understanding of the correct legal source. The advocate also needs to relate the facts and the relevant legal sources. One technique for doing this, suggested by Sherr, is to draw up a skeleton map of law and facts.[8] The skeleton map provides a quick guide to the arguments in support of the client's case.

A skeleton map of law and facts

Here is an example of a skeleton map of law and facts for the case of a client who has been disqualified from receiving unemployment benefit.

Item	Law	Relevant facts and proof
1	Dismissal by employer	Letter dated 11/5/94 confirming dismissal for poor timekeeping.
2	Claim for benefit	Claim form dated 12/5/94 making a claim for unemployment benefit.
3	Disqualification	Letter dated 13/6/94 disqualifying client from benefit.
4	Employment not lost through misconduct	Client given no warning of poor timekeeping. Firm in financial trouble and looking to reduce workforce. Client's memory

| 5 | If disqualification not lifted, should be for a minimal period and not the full 26 weeks (R (U) 4/87). | indicates that he was only late 40 per cent of the time. This is the first such 'offence'. The alleged misconduct is at the lower end of the scale. Client is experiencing hardship and is finding it hard to get another job because of dismissal. If client had been employed over two years, this would be unfair dismissal.[9] |

Unless you are successful in negotiations or through preliminary written advocacy, the next step may be litigation.

References

1   *Annual Report of the Chief Adjudication Officer for 1991–92 on Adjudication Standards* (1992), London: HMSO.
2   Commission for Local Administration for England (1991), *Report into Maladministration by Essex County Council.*
3   Lord Hailsham's 1983 Hamlyn Lecture, cited in Tunkel, V. (1992), *Legal Research*, London: Blackstone Press.
4   James, J. S. (1986), *Stroud's Judicial Dictionary*, London: Sweet and Maxwell.
5   Saunders, J. B. (ed.) (1969), *Words and Phrases Legally Defined*, London: Butterworth.
6   Maxwell, P. R. (1969), *The Interpretation of Statutes*, London: Sweet and Maxwell.
7   R (U) 4/87.
8   As described by Sherr, A. (1993), *Advocacy*, London: Blackstone Press.
9   Ibid. (adapted).

10 Litigation

'Litigation' is the term used to describe the process of presenting the client's case to an arbitrator, normally by an oral presentation, as opposed to direct negotiation or correspondence with the other side. It may involve other types of advocacy apart from litigation before a court or tribunal. Litigation may include representation before complaints panels or disciplinary hearings, or it might involve less formal presentations to a senior official or a case conference, although, where clear formal channels of appeal and challenge exist, these should normally be used as a better result will often be obtained. 'Soft' forms of litigation such as case conferences will have less structure, and some of the more formal and legalistic parts of this chapter will not apply. However, there will still be a large degree of common ground in the skills used when acting as an advocate in any setting. Litigation is used in advocacy because it can be effective. It can be easier to persuade a third party acting as an arbitrator than the other side, who may be unable or unwilling to agree with the apparent rightness or logic of the advocate's arguments.

To lawyers, advocacy is the process of representing and acting in court. Much of this chapter has been adapted from the techniques used by lawyers in a manner which is relevant for other advocates, and it is not a full exposition of the subject.

In some cases litigation will be in the client's best interests; at other times it can indicate a failure of earlier efforts, for many reasons, and not necessarily because of an incorrect approach by the advocate. Litigation can involve having to delay the final outcome – but then so can negotiation. While delay may be off-putting for some clients and it can add to their anxiety, it should not be avoided for those reasons unless there really is a major risk of the client coming to harm as a result of the delay. In such cases it would be worth obtaining specialist advice on how to progress.

Litigation can be used in some cases as a creative part of advocacy. For example, there is little to be lost by appealing against refusals of housing where internal appeal mechanisms exist. In the case of benefits, there is hardly ever anything to be lost. Sometimes litigation can be used as a means to protect a client – such as when one submits an appeal against recovery of overpaid benefit. Repayments from the client's benefit should stop, and the client's standard of living can be protected while research is undertaken. Litigation can also be used as a lever to force the other side to produce sensitive information or internal papers to justify their actions. It is more difficult to achieve this without any form of litigation as one will be reliant on the other side's goodwill. Often when some form of litigation is commenced, the matter is passed up the management line and greater expertise is brought to bear on the problem. This often leads to a resolution.

In cases affecting many clients, simultaneous mass litigation can be a highly effective technique. The other side may back down in the face of the workload caused by so many clients and, in a marginal argument, it may be easier for them to settle in full rather than argue each case. There are, of course, many other arguments in favour of litigating a matter, and it is an option which must always be considered.

Litigation can be complex and there is a need for technical knowledge about the procedures to be used. Advocates must recognise the limits of their expertise and call upon appropriate help. However, the restrictions on Legal Aid and the underfunding of good advice agencies and advisers means that often it may be a matter of a client's trade union representative, social worker or housing officer acting as advocate in some form of litigation. It is therefore fitting that this chapter should begin with a few words of warning and some of encouragement.

Do not attempt to represent before a hearing, court or tribunal if you feel very unconfident about doing so. Try to get an expert to do it with you or, if all else fails, try to observe similar proceedings. Do not represent unless you have researched all the relevant legal and procedural issues. The depth of research needed will vary from hearing to hearing, and will depend on the type of case. A representation about a care issue at a case conference will need less technical knowledge than representing a tenant in court in possession proceedings. However, even the latter can be tackled successfully with the right support and back-up. For example, one can make use of written arguments prepared by an expert.

If the hearing will involve questioning of witnesses, there are particular techniques that must be applied. It is not a matter of firing off a few salvos at the other side's witness and copying a television court-room drama. There may be flaws in the procedure that produce an unsatisfactory result for the client and which require specialist skills to resolve. Alternatively, the other side may ambush you with surprising new arguments or evidence. Do not go into any type of litigation unless you are sure of where you stand.

The positive side of litigation is that it can produce a very good result for the client, often far better than anything that can be obtained through other means. Indeed, one of the measures when considering negotiation is to assess what the likely result of litigation would be, and to set this result as a target for negotiation. There is also a growing readiness to accept representation by non-lawyers. Certainly the place of lay advocates is now well-accepted at tribunals, and in the courts it is spreading. In particular, with debt and housing matters, courts are increasingly able to accept advocates in human service organisations as effectively having a full right of audience, and procedures are being simplified to enable this to occur. However, local practices do vary, and enquiries on this formality to the clerk to the court should be made in advance.

Similarly, there is a trend for the development of complaints and appeal panels on housing, health and social services matters. It is unlikely that this trend will be reversed as it is a more effective way for organisations to hear the concerns of consumers, and it will often be cheaper than not having such panels as the alternative may be serious litigation in the courts. In practice, professional representation will usually not be available for such panels and a lay advocate will have to take on the role of representative.

It is also the case that the skills of lawyers on welfare issues are sadly lacking. This is quite widely acknowledged and is a reflection of the commercial leanings of the legal profession. It is also highly unlikely that a lawyer will have the necessary time or skill to represent on care-related unbounded problems and, unless they are specialists, their work on the more bounded, legalistic welfare issues can be poor. In many cases, it is possible for lay advocates to be very effective provided they have access to good support systems and to independent expertise. Some organisations have in-house welfare rights and other specialists who can provide such support, or there may be effective specialist agencies in the locality which can provide it.

There is also the question of costs. Litigation may involve the client in expense. If they are able to get Legal Aid this may be less of a problem, but in most debt cases, for example, the advocate will be admitting the other side's right to the money but disputing the rate of repayment. Certain costs may also be added to the debt unless it is possible to have the costs reduced by the court 'taxing' them (i.e. examining them in detail – a useful procedure), or if it can be shown that the litigation was unnecessary as the client's offer to pay was accepted by the court. In the case of tribunals, complaints panels and internal hearings, there will not be any costs for the client, and most should even pay for the client's travel and other expenses. If they don't pay, this is something which ought to be pursued.

Preliminaries

Before embarking on litigation, there are a number of preliminary considerations. Good preparation is essential. Hopefully, this will largely have been covered through legal research. Full details of the procedural aspects of a hearing should be obtained as part of the legal research. Even mundane aspects of these can raise important points for or against the client.

Preparation checklist

1 Examine the written evidence and study the paperwork. Is everything included – especially from the other side? Are there extracts from files, case notes, letters, claim forms, records of phone calls? When were notes made, and by whom? Insist on the other side producing a written submission of their case in good time and in advance of a hearing. Do you have copies of books or guidance on the hearing's procedure?

2 What is the essential basis of the argument?

3 Study the relevant legislation and caselaw. Are any other legal principles relevant? Check internal policy and procedures and standards statements. Apply principles of interpretation and reasoning. Try to establish the logical basis of your argument as it relates to the facts.

4 Do you need more information or facts?

5 What proof is there for the facts and arguments you will advance?

6 What will witnesses say? Are they reliable? How will you prepare witnesses you will be using? Will they perform well? Would sworn witness statements be useful in less formal hearings?

7 When the other side have completed their submission, will they have made their case adequately? What weaknesses exist in the arguments?

8 What flaws are there in your arguments? What contrary evidence might be produced? Have you gone through your arguments with a colleague for a second opinion?

9 What do you know about the background of witnesses?

10 Put yourself in the other side's shoes and run through their arguments.

11 Have you written a submission setting out your arguments? It does add to preparation time, but a written submission has more impact and helps others to focus on the core of your case.[1]

Beware the danger of bias. This applies particularly to less formal hearings and appeal panels. The principles of natural justice should normally be observed, which means that there should be clear distinctions between the members of the panel, any specialist adviser and the other side. It is far from unknown for the other side to have a colleague on the panel or to have prior discussions with the panel or the adviser. There have even been instances where the other side has sat in with the panel while the client is absent. If there would be a risk of bias in such cases, it should be pointed out as soon as it occurs.

The next preliminary matter is to check what formalities exist for litigation before the court, tribunal or hearing. This will include seating arrangements and dress. You should object to seating arrangements which put you and the client at a disadvantage to the other side. Your appearance shouldn't matter, but it often does. Litigation and protection of the rights of clients is a serious matter, and appearances can detract from this and irritate the people one is appearing before. Don't unnecessarily jeopardise your client's case by wearing inappropriate clothing. This is more likely to be an issue where the litigation involves a court, but it can also apply to more informal hearings. Similarly, remember titles and correct forms of address before even the most mundane hearings. The hearing will be before a body with power and influence, and respect for that power will place you in a more powerful position to help the client.

Finally, time may be of the essence. There are often time limits for submitting appeals and also for appealing against the decision of a first-stage appeal. Be aware of them. Some appeal panels may have no formal appeals procedure, but action may be taken in the High Court. Again there are time limits and delay should be avoided.

One of the major pieces of litigation relevant to advocacy on welfare-related matters is judicial review. This procedure requires skilled legal representation, but lay advocates are often the first to identify the possibility of such an action in an individual case. Judicial review is a procedure in the High Court (or Court of Session in Scotland) which enables the actions of public bodies (and many private bodies) to be challenged. It may be possible to challenge the decisions of appeals panels and similar bodies by judicial review, and very important extensions of the rights of people who use public welfare services have emerged from its use. The use of judicial review is most marked in housing matters (particularly in homelessness), but it has been used successfully in immigration, social security, social services and health matters.

A specialist text such as Wade's *Administrative Law*[2] should be consulted for more details, but the following principles should be remembered as a pointer to when to obtain specialist legal advice on judicial review:

1   The body has exceeded its jurisdiction or authority.
2   The body's powers have been exercised by the wrong person.
3   The correct procedure has not been followed.
4   The body may have taken the wrong type of decision. This can apply if the decision of the body could be viewed as adopting the wrong interpretation of the law.

5   The body may be exercising its powers in the wrong circumstances.
6   The body may have taken irrelevant considerations into account in reaching its decision.
7   The body may have used its powers for an improper purpose.
8   The body may have acted in bad faith.
9   The body may have acted unreasonably.

Two further general principles can be relevant when bodies carry out formal appeals or hearings, but there are exceptions in the types of hearings to which they apply:

10   The hearing has given a reasonable suspicion of bias or an arbitrator has an interest in either side's case.
11   There must be an adequate opportunity for both sides to prepare their case, present their case, and for parties to be represented.

These last two principles are the basis of the rules of 'natural justice'.

Talking and persuading

The advocate's presentation of the case is significant, although it is difficult to say how far a weak case is turned around by good presentation or a strong case lost by bad presentation. However, poor presentation certainly does not help, and it is important to emphasise the strengths of the facts in your case and the logic and reasoning of the arguments in your client's favour. There will usually be a running order to the hearing itself. The standard format for a running order is:

1   Opening statement on behalf of the person bringing the case
2   Examination of evidence and witnesses brought by this party
3   Opening statement by the other party
4   Examination of their evidence and witnesses
5   Re-examination if new evidence has emerged
6   Closing statements – perhaps including any necessary points of mitigation

However, procedures will vary and in tribunals and appeal or complaints hearings the procedure will be more fluid and investigatory, rather than adversarial.

The opening statement is an important part of any presentation. You should make clear your goals, what you expect the hearing to decide, and why. This may also be the time to use the chronology of facts – especially if these are unlikely to be controversial. Your skeleton map (see pp. 127–8) is also useful at this stage. Be concise and remember that you are addressing the hearing, not the other side, so you should make a point of establishing eye contact with all members of a tribunal or panel and not just the person chairing it or one who seems sympathetic. Above all, you have to persuade. Persuasion is best achieved by precise, clear speech. It is also helped by speaking assertively and politely to the hearing, and by not saying too much – which can be difficult as you are likely to be on edge. More cases have been lost by saying too much than have been lost by saying too little.

There are a number of characteristics to effective speaking, including:

- Avoid the use of hand movements.
- Avoid using gestures.
- Adopt a sincere and clear tone.
- Ensure your arguments appear well prepared.
- Point out helpful factual evidence (make sure everyone has copies).
- Ensure your speech has a clear structure, starting with the specific and then moving to the general.
- Avoid losing patience with the other side no matter how infuriating or insulting they become.
- Although it is difficult to write while speaking, you should have your arguments set out in note form and you should make a careful note of what is said by others.

Persuasion also involves convincing the panel, court or tribunal that your case is right and the other side is wrong. At times this will be easy as the other side will have simply made a mistake (a linear problem) but does not wish to admit it. At other times you will have to show that your interpretation is superior to that of the other side. To a large extent this is something which comes with experience. It helps if you can demonstrate the logical flow of your thoughts, and that there is a clear distinction between your argument and that put forward by the other side.

In case where the case revolves around the circumstances of the client, it can be powerful to try the 'Look at the person' approach. Care must be exercised as this could easily humiliate the client but, where it is relevant, it can be powerful if used selectively to point out the absurdity of the other side's position. The 'Look at the person' approach can be useful where you are trying to convince someone of the need to exercise discretion in your client's favour, but it is unlikely to work where the case merely involves argument on the correct legal or procedural interpretation to be applied. However, it usually doesn't do any harm to elicit sympathy and, if nothing else, it can make a hostile arbitrator less so. Clearly, the client's instructions will be needed in this respect.

If you are representing before a case conference or a complaints panel, it is especially helpful to show how the other side may not have followed their own policies or procedures, or that those policies and procedures are unreasonable, incorrect or inappropriate. It can also be very useful to think in advance of how to appeal to enlightened self-interest on the part of the other side, as well as other ways in which your seemingly absurd suggestions can be accommodated as being consistent with their other actions; or alternatively, how your argument might mean that old, outdated practices can be altered if a new approach is taken. To establish how persuasive your case is it is always helpful to run through the arguments with a colleague.

Persuasion exercise

This is a very simple exercise in persuasion. You will need a partner to practise on.

You have ten minutes to persuade your partner that bicycles are a superior form of transport to motor cars. Before starting, spend a few minutes sketching out your arguments and anticipate all the counter-arguments. These might include convenience, speed, safety, economic impact, environmental aspects, etc.

There will usually be an opportunity for a closing statement. Normally you should not introduce any new arguments at this point but you can comment adversely on points raised by the other side. The closing remarks should again clearly define the issues and what is being asked for. There should be positive support for your client's case rather than concentration on the weaknesses of the other side's case, and the manner in which it is carried out should be appropriate, as explained earlier in this chapter.

Witnesses and evidence

It can often be necessary to use evidence to support your arguments. Evidence may be presented in the form of letters or statements from others, or directly from questioning someone as a witness. Usually the evidence in the type of litigation which concerns advocates in human service organisations is not complex or open to dispute. Evidence in any formal sense is more likely to apply when the litigation involves a court or tribunal, but it can also be important in less formal complaints and appeal panels.

Evidence can present problems, and witnesses can be a particular stumbling-block. The use of evidence and witnesses is a highly refined skill at which lawyers often excel. Once again, that expertise may not be on hand,

and you will have to do your best in the circumstances. In court settings, there are also detailed rules governing evidence; however, in tribunals and less formal appeals or litigation, these do not apply, and informality makes the process simpler for both the client and their representative.

Where evidence is to be produced which is in paper form, a number of basics should be attended to:

1   It may be possible to get an expert evidence report in support of your case via the Legal Aid scheme. This could include independent medical, environmental health, building condition or valuation reports. Such evidence will be important to rebut any apparently strong evidence from the other side.
2   Any statements should be in the form of sworn affidavits. Where less formal rules of evidence apply, a statement need not be sworn but should still be properly laid out, with an opening sentence making it clear that it is a statement from a particular person, giving their address and credentials (even if this is just a character reference, one needs to state how long the person has known the client and in what capacity).
3   Produce the evidence in advance of any hearing to reduce the chances of an adjournment.
4   Try to avoid submitting points which are unsupported by any evidence. If nothing else, the client should be able to confirm what you say.
5   Be particularly careful not to give evidence yourself, and make it clear which facts are not within your direct knowledge.

As stated earlier, witnesses pose a particular problem, and this includes the client as a witness. It is hard to predict how someone will perform as a witness, and appearances can be deceptive. Witnesses can be used in a variety of litigation settings, and some will be less stressful for them than others, but always discuss with your witnesses what they are going to say. Don't put words into their mouth, but leading them through their evidence before the hearing is an important safeguard and enables you to be forewarned of possible problems.

This may not be possible if the other side produces witnesses. With the other side's witnesses in particular, avoid asking a question if you don't know the answer. It is also better to ask few rather than too many questions, and try to have written notes of what you want to ask. You should be clear about what you are trying to achieve, and ask questions which are more likely to produce answers in support of your proposition. A nineteenth-century US lawyer, David Paul Brown, devised a number of rules now known as Brown's Rules for dealing with witnesses. They are useful in whatever setting the litigation occurs.[3]

Brown's rules: a summary

1   When a witness is forward or impertinent, be serious and very grave with them.
2   When a witness is timid or nervous, begin by asking them questions about familiar matters and proceed only gradually to contentious questions.
3   When a witness is unfavourable and their evidence has set you back, conceal your shock or frustration.
4   When a witness is prejudiced against your client, get rid of them as soon as possible.
5   When a witness is to be called by the other side, let them call them rather than you, as you may have at least two chances to question them.
6   Never ask a witness a question without an objective.

I do not propose to go into the rules about admissibility of evidence. These are relevant to court settings, but are less of a problem in tribunals and less formal hearings. One form of evidence which can sometimes be disputed is 'hearsay evidence'. This is evidence which is not within the direct knowledge of the person giving it. For example, 'Mrs Smith told me that she saw him pick up the book.' Such evidence can be admissible in court in certain limited circumstances, and it is admissible at tribunals, but it should not be given as much weight as direct evidence and, if it is used by the other side and it is unhelpful, the inherent unreliability of the evidence should be pointed out. Hearsay evidence is much more likely to be used at less formal hearings and panels. Its value can work for or against the client.

While much of this and the previous chapter has concentrated upon some of the more legalistic aspects of advocacy by human service professions, it does illustrate the range of skills needed for effective advocacy by human service professionals. Indeed, if some of the 'softer', less formal types of advocacy were to develop the 'harder', more legalistic approach, the client could benefit. I know from my own experience that many situations where someone has attempted to act as an advocate have been undermined by applying irrelevant and improper procedures, effectively denying the client a voice. The development of skills in advocacy will enable us to *give* the client a voice, and ensure that the services they need are made answerable and relevant.

References

1   Adapted from Sherr, A. (1993), *Advocacy*, London: Blackstone Press.
2   Wade, H. W. R. (1988), *Administrative Law*, Oxford University Press.
3   Cited in Murphy, P. (1990), *Evidence and Advocacy*, London: Blackstone Press.

11 A structure for advocacy

This chapter demonstrates how the skills of advocacy interrelate and how these different skills can be applied at various stages of the advocacy process. This process applies whether the advocate is dealing with a bounded or an unbounded problem. As has become clear, effective advocacy must have a structure, and failure to recognise that structure or to apply relevant skills at each stage will often mean that the advocacy is not successful. Advocacy is a dynamic process, and distinct stages can be identified in the advocacy on each case. At each stage a different level and type of skill is needed, though some skills are common to several stages.

While at first sight some of this might seem overawing to the novice, and while it also seems to prolong matters, identification of the stages and use of the right mix of skills and ethical principles will actually save time in the long run. How often have advocates effectively wasted theirs and the client's time by not proceeding in an organised and consistent manner?

Sadly, the lack of understanding of advocacy skills, and the assumption that successful advocacy is merely a combination of force of personality and good technical knowledge, mean that the structure of advocacy may be ignored, consequently undermining the efforts of the advocate who applies inappropriate skills at different stages, or who omits stages.

Advocacy is essentially an interactive process involving three parties: client, advocate and the other side. Recognition of the structure of any interactive process helps make it tangible, easier to understand and quantify. It removes the mystique and, by helping clients understand the structure, the process becomes less mysterious and more empowering.

In cases where advocacy occurs, one can identify up to six clear stages. There is no particular timescale for each stage, but each must be worked through using the right mix of skills if there is to be a satisfactory outcome.

The stages of advocacy

Stage 1: Presentation of the problem – where a problem requiring advocacy is presented or discovered by the advocate.

Stage 2: Information-gathering – gathering relevant information and obtaining instructions from the client.

Stage 3: Legal research – comparing the facts with legal, policy or procedural sources.

Stage 4: Interpretation and feedback to the client – analysing the facts and legal sources and forming a judgement about the nature of the problem, the best approach to be used and obtaining further facts and instructions if necessary; reaching a conclusion about whether to go to stage 5 or to stage 6.

Stage 5: Active negotiation and advocacy – undertaking the necessary negotiations and/or preliminary advocacy with the other side.

Stage 6: Litigation – use of formal appeals and other mechanisms to achieve the objective if stage 5 is either not appropriate or successful.

The stages

Take a recent example of advocacy in which you have been involved. Map out a rough plan of the events that took place and see if you can identify stages in the advocacy. If the advocacy was not as effective as you had hoped, was it because you jumped stages or rushed through them without full use of the skills needed to get to the next stage?

Stage 1: Presentation of the problem

Unfortunately, people and their problems seldom arrive in neat packages. Sometimes a client will present you with a problem that clearly requires advocacy – the clear denial of rights, or a dispute involving a regulated system are obvious examples. At other times a problem will only emerge as part of a human service professional's other work with a client. This is not the case with paid advocates such as advice workers or lawyers: most of the time their clients will approach them because they recognise that there is a problem which requires someone to act for them. Many consumers of welfare services have little concept of their rights because the prevailing culture denies those rights, and the systems which they face can appear to be omnipotent.

Advocates need effective interviewing and listening skills to ensure that a problem is presented, or to uncover a problem that needs advocacy but which is hidden among other issues. They also need sufficient technical knowledge to tell whether a problem is one which is best served by advocacy – this may be no more than a hunch that something is wrong and that someone is being denied something they ought to have. There is also a skill in recognising this when there is a bombardment of other issues and problems which *don't* need advocacy. In such situations it is easy for advocacy to be marginalised, as it may not be viewed as central to the professional's 'main' task. However, advocacy is concerned with obtaining money, better housing, services and treatment, without which a person cannot function adequately. Indeed, the failure to meet such basic needs is often the underlying cause of many health and inter-personal problems. If it is not the cause, it will certainly worsen matters. In addition, an understanding of the ethical principles of advocacy – primarily Principle 1, 'Act in the client's best interests' – may subconsciously motivate a human service professional to identify the need for advocacy when a problem is presented.

Stage 2: Information-gathering

Having become aware of a problem that requires advocacy, the next stage is to gather facts. The importance of this was discussed earlier, and it demonstrates the need for a methodical approach, rather than instantly springing into action and becoming involved in active advocacy with the other side. It is equally important to gather information from the other side, as their perception and factual recall can mean that you need to alter your tactics; when doing so, it is important to note any adverse comments made about the client, or any views expressed by the other side which are based on prejudice, coincidence or bad practice. These can be important in demonstrating the incorrectness of the other side's approach, and may also form the basis of a formal complaint designed to address the wider problem of attitudes or practices, which may affect others as well as the client. For example, negative remarks about the client by benefits officials may indicate prejudice towards a particular type of person, and negative remarks by care staff may indicate a need for training or better management control. They may also form the basis of a complaint to an ombudsman or, in more serious instances, a claim for damages because of the obvious bad faith exhibited in refusing to assist the client.

It will be necessary to secure the client's consent to obtain information from other people. As a matter of course you should draw up a standard letter giving such consent, but some organisations will divulge information to an advocate by phone if it is made clear that you are acting on behalf of a client. Sometimes the insistence on written consent can be used as a block on effective advocacy – particularly advocacy which needs to be undertaken in haste. Use of the fax machine is one way round this problem, as is the agreement of a protocol with the other side for the conduct of advocacy.

The phone can be very helpful in gathering information. It can often be necessary to ask supplementary questions when trying to establish the full facts of a case, and also in response to the answers given to the opening questions. This is difficult to do by letter, and the inevitable delays of the postal system effectively rule this out as impractical. At this stage it is very important to avoid actually advocating for the client until the other stages have been reached.

The type of information needed will vary from case to case, and will depend upon the nature of the problem. Chapter 3's case-studies of advocacy in specific areas contained lists of the range of information needed. Obtaining this information first time round saves a lot of time, and will help in securing a quick resolution. During this stage you could also construct a chronology and the beginning of a skeleton map (see pp. 127–8).

It may be necessary to act assertively to obtain the information needed, but it should not be necessary to use aggression in a constructive manner. The other side may become defensive when the advocate starts to make enquiries, as it can signal the start of a challenge to something they have done. Assertive behaviour is an effective way of coping with such defensiveness but, in some cases, the other side may actively obstruct the advocate from obtaining information – sadly it does happen, and a more robust approach will be needed.

Good information-gathering will require effective time management skills and a degree of creative thinking when trying to establish what secondary supporting information is needed to enhance a case. Effective information-gathering will also help time management throughout the conduct of a case, and it will reduce stress by ensuring that, as far as is reasonably practicable, a major, solid piece of work has been undertaken at the outset to lessen the risk of failure and subsequent frustration.

Often, having obtained sufficient facts, it is clear that more detail is needed – perhaps expert medical evidence or detailed information from creditors' financial records. However, even with a few factual gaps, it may still be possible to form a safe provisional view of the overall factual picture which will enable the next stage to be approached with confidence.

Stage 3: Legal research

Chapter 9 explained legal research and its breadth. Clearly it is impossible to conduct any legal research until you have gathered facts and information, and insufficient facts could lead you to research the wrong issue, producing less effective advocacy and wasting time. One major consideration at this stage is that the better your technical knowledge about the area, the more successful you will be. If your knowledge is poor but you still obtain a positive result, this may blind you to the objective effectiveness of your advocacy. Without being aware of gaps in your expertise it is impossible to assess how effective you might otherwise have been. By the time this stage is complete, there should be a complete skeleton map and you should have formed a judgement about:

- The type of problem (bounded or unbounded)
- The most effective approach or remedy
- The chances of success for the client
- The legal and factual issues involved
- The gaps in the case

Having reached a judgement, the next stage enables you to formulate an action plan.

Stage 4: Interpretation and feedback to the client

At this stage, having reached a judgement about which tactics and issues to pursue, you should give feedback to the client and obtain their views on how to proceed. Failure to do this not only means that you are not engaging the client in the process, which means the client is unlikely to learn from the experience or be motivated and empowered, but your interpretation of the issues may be at variance with the client's, or the client may not wish to pursue the remedies proposed. In addition, further information may be needed from the client. For example, a case involving the non-provision of suitable care by a social services department might be capable of resolution in the following ways:

1 Negotiation to achieve the required level and type of care for a client
2 Court action to force the provision of care
3 Negotiation to provide care, with a clear understanding that legal action will be taken if the care is not provided

4   Use of a complaints procedure
5   A request that the care be provided – the social services department may not know about all the care needs, or may not have carried out an assessment of the needs
6   A complaint to the Local Government Ombudsman – particularly if the failure to provide care is accompanied by poor service or inadequate responses to representations

These courses of action involve varying levels of risk for the client, and you need to seek their agreement about the approach to be taken.

At this stage you will need to use the correct interviewing skills – appropriate language and explanations are very important. In a few cases, the matters will be much clearer and there may not be a need for a formal interview as such. Self-management skills are relevant here because this stage should be regarded as an essential element of each piece of advocacy, and this requires good time management. A degree of creative thinking may also be needed to find the right solution or interpretation. In some cases, writing skills will come to the fore, as it can be helpful to provide the client with a written summary of the issues and the proposed course of action.

The interpretation and feedback stage is also useful for determining the client's views on the other side's interpretation of the factual and legal issues – especially where there are any discrepancies in the facts. Explaining a matter to the client will always be valuable, as the very process of doing so helps you to clarify your thoughts further and to be even more creative.

When the matter has been fed back to the client and everyone is clear about what is to be done, the next step is to do it!

Stage 5: Active negotiation and advocacy

As I have indicated before, you should avoid undertaking advocacy on an individual case without the relevant skills or without adopting a structured approach. A frequent problem with advocacy by human service professionals is that they are presented with a problem and almost immediately proceed to negotiate with the other side. As a result the advocacy can be frustrating and ineffective. This is because the advocate is acting without all the facts, without the right legal research, and probably without the client's full consent. This approach is not only bad practice, but is at variance with the ethical principles of advocacy.

You should now be clear about the approach to be used and the type of problem involved – bounded or unbounded. As stated earlier, the appropriate course of action will be determined by the urgency, the seriousness, the remedies available and the degree of structure in the problem, as well as the ethical principles underlying your whole approach. At the active stage you may be negotiating or trying to persuade the other side to alter course. Constructively channelled aggression may be needed, as well as assertion skills. Any verbal contact should be noted, and any points agreed orally should be followed up in writing. And, of course, at this stage you will be making full use of all your negotiating skills.

The other side may respond in a manner which requires time for reflection or further research, in which case you need to go back a stage or two and forward again to the active stage. This highlights the need for a clear, structured approach, and the need to think and act methodically to get the best result. Quick, off-the-cuff responses are seldom the most effective.

Of course, this assumes that you get a response from the other side at all. It is far from unknown for the other side to ignore requests to take a particular course of action. You need a system to follow up written and other requests, and to make sure that responses are obtained. Never accept silence – it is bad practice, both for the advocate and the other side.

At the active stage you may get the best result for the client. Either you will achieve everything by the robust advocacy and arguments put forward and the other side will be aware of the strength of your position, or a negotiated settlement will have been obtained, if the problem was incapable of resolution by a more litigious approach. In other cases, the result will be negative, inconclusive or an attempt to compromise. The advocate's duty does not extend to reaching a compromise: the duty is to obtain the best result for the client. Compromises can seem attractive and conciliatory, but they are rarely the best that could have been obtained if a different approach had been used. This obviously applies to problems governed by a regulated system – bounded problems – but it can also apply to unbounded problems. In the case of the latter, the approach to negotiation discussed later means that a more constructive and creative approach is adopted, rather than an approach based upon weakness implied in the desire to reach a compromise.

If the result is not sufficient at this stage, you will need to proceed to the next and final stage.

Stage 6: Litigation

As I indicated in Chapter 10, in the context of advocacy by human service professionals, litigation is not confined to action in courts and tribunals – even though not enough use is made of these forums in legal issues affecting those on low incomes. Litigation can also involve taking a matter to an ombudsman, to a complaints panel or to a case conference. Its distinguishing feature is that it involves addressing an arbitrator, rather than dialogue with the other side.

Litigation often looks daunting and legalistic, and often it is, but it is essential if the results obtained earlier are insufficient. It may be that a more skilled person than the average human service professional has to take on this stage of the advocacy. The important thing is that it is known to be an option and that it is considered. Neglecting this final, and often most thorough, way of achieving the best for the client is akin to preparing a meal carefully and then serving it uncooked.

One of the essential skills of a human service professional engaged in advocacy is to identify people who can undertake litigation in various forms, and to develop appropriate referral mechanisms. Alternatively, it may be possible to undertake some litigation yourself, with access to consultancy and advice or in partnership with a more skilled person.

Of course, not all litigation succeeds but, to have reached this stage, everything else must also have failed, and the reality for most clients is that the remedies available often involve little or no cost, they have little to lose, and the mere fact that the other side has been challenged rigorously means that they are more likely to work at getting things right for other clients. Finally, any form of litigation means that a rights-based perspective may be brought to bear on matters which may not always have been regarded as areas where people *have* rights. If these rights are meaningful, they will be capable of enforcement – sometimes against the wishes of the other side. Litigation is the process of enforcement.

The stages of advocacy illustrated

The following case-study illustrates the stages of action and the range of skills which are relevant in a simple problem encountered quite often by people working in a variety of settings. It is a classic bounded problem – which makes illustration simpler.

An unemployed couple with two young children receive their benefit cheque every two weeks on a Friday. This Friday it has not arrived so they go to a local advice centre.

Stage 1: Presentation

The clients tell an advice worker that their payment hasn't arrived and that they have no money. They have been in touch with the benefit office, who have told them that they must wait three working days before they can replace the cheque.

Stage 2: Information-gathering

The advice worker gathers certain details – for example, details of the family members, their health problems and financial situation. It emerges that the family have debts and they are in rent arrears. If they miss a payment off the arrears the local authority landlord have said they will apply for a warrant to evict them as they have a suspended Possession Order on the property. This thus reveals other problems which were not apparent at the presentation stage and which will need further work at a later date. The advice worker informs the clients that the priority has to be to get them a payment.

Stage 3: Legal research

The advice worker consults a standard reference book and also obtains a second opinion from a colleague. They come to the conclusion that the correct legal position is that the payment is due, and that in law this means the benefit office owe the clients that money. Legal action to obtain the payment could be used. The local social services department also have a legal duty to assist financially in such cases. The tactics are thus to ask for an immediate replacement, if this fails, to issue proceedings, and also to ask social services to make a payment. It will also be necessary to prevent the landlord taking action.

Stage 4: Interpretation and feedback

The advice worker informs the clients of the various legal and tactical options. The clients are worried about legal action in case the benefit office take it out on them in some way. They had an unpleasant interview with them when they first claimed and they don't want this repeated. The advice worker tells them that this is unlikely and, if there was any evidence of revenge, she would act to defend the couple's interests with the fullest possible force.

The clients are also worried that referring matters to social services might mean the children being taken into care. The advice worker again reassures them that this should not happen solely because they have no money this week, that the primary duty is to prevent children being taken into care, and there are legal safeguards to enforce this. The clients agree that the advice worker's suggested course of action should be followed.

A further appointment will be needed to discuss the debts, and an approach will also have to made to the landlord.

Stage 5: Active negotiation and advocacy

The advice worker phones the benefit office with the clients present. She asks to speak to a member of the management staff. The advice worker points out the family's circumstances and asks for an immediate payment. The manager says he will investigate and ring back. The advice worker agrees that this can be done, and that the return phone call will be within ten minutes.

The manager's assistant phones back to confirm that a payment was put in the post but appears either not to have arrived or to have been stolen. He says that this has happened before to these clients. They will not make a payment, but they might be able to make a crisis loan to the clients. The advice worker tells the benefit office that, if no payment is made, legal action to secure the payment will have to be taken. A crisis loan is not acceptable as the client will have to pay back money they are owed by the benefit office. The advice worker then telephones the local authority landlord and explains the problem with the benefit cheque. The member of staff to whom she speaks confirms that no action will be taken in the circumstances. The advice worker sends a letter by post confirming this agreement.

Stage 6: Litigation

The advice worker sends a letter to the benefit office's solicitors and a copy to the manager, advising that unless payment is made within two working days a summons will be issued. She also rings the local social services and informs them of the situation and of the need for a cash payment. The social worker on duty to whom she speaks is reluctant, but agrees to a payment when it is pointed out that there are specific duties in such a case.

The clients receive a payment from the local office the next working day, together with an apology as there had been a computer error which stopped their payment going out.

12 Epilogue: Where to from here?

A book concerned with a practical skill such as advocacy is only as good as the use made of it and the results that follow. While advocacy has been around for a long time and is used with varying degrees of success by many people, it has not hitherto been regarded as an activity which needs particular skills. If there is now a recognition of these skills – even if you disagree with the approach taken – readers will have done something positive with this material. Others can and should add to the debate and the body of knowledge in this area.

Advocacy can also be limited in its effects by being too closely linked to individualism. Most of the problems which advocates resolve will be faced by hundreds of thousands of other people. Not only can advocacy take on a collective form, but it is more effective if used as part of a wider strategy for helping others. This can range from the other side learning lessons from the way individual cases were dealt with to taking a test-case approach, or to courting publicity as a means of strengthening the impact of your arguments.

But none of this will bear fruit unless you actually apply the skills outlined in this book and unless you adopt the systematic and structured approaches described. So the first resolution for any reader has to be that you will *use* the material. If it doesn't work, or if you find a better way of doing it, tell me and tell others. Do the same if it does work and your success rate increases.

You should also remember that, while advocacy skills, a sound understanding of ethics and a clear sense of purpose and structure are very important, technical and legal knowledge about the area in which you are acting are essential. The better your knowledge, the better your advocacy skills and the greater your impact. Good advocacy or negotiating skills will not compensate for a lack of the appropriate knowledge. Equally, it must be recognised that one of the reasons why advocacy has not been regarded as

149

requiring particular skills is the frequent emphasis on technical or legal knowledge, which then becomes a substitute for adequate advocacy skills.

Advocates must also recognise that their actions may challenge organisations' cultural norms. The other side may feel threatened by your actions. They may try to personalise matters or be difficult in various ways. Avoid reciprocating, and take matters further formally if this situation arises. The advocate who acts vigorously in pursuit of the client's case is only seeking the same rights for the client which those with money and influence enjoy daily. Experience also shows that persistence does pay off. Not only may you get the result you intended, but respect often follows for the advocate who is resolute and knowledgeable. And at the end of the day, your primary ethical obligation is to the client rather than the sensitivities of the other side.

In recent years, the acknowledgement by those running welfare bureaucracies that they must listen to their customers and strive to meet their needs puts the advocate in a strong position. Organisations which are too internally focused and defensive about the representations of customers are unlikely to prosper. Advocates of such customers can only benefit from this cultural change which sees customers as central to the organisations' purpose. The signs are also that this cultural change in organisations is unlikely to disappear. And, if customer rights and charters are worth the paper they are written on, someone must be there to act as an advocate to enforce those rights, to give voice to the customer's needs, and to point out the organisations' failure to meet those needs.

Such activity requires the mix of ethics, skills and structure described in this book.

Bibliography

The following books provide useful guidance and help on advocacy and some go into more detail about the skills used by advocates.

Background to advocacy

Hyam, J. (1990), *Advocacy Skills*, London: Stephens.
The MIND Guide to advocacy – Empowerment in Action (1992), London: MIND Publications.
Pannick, D. (1993), *Advocates*, Oxford University Press.
Read, J. and Wallcraft, J. (1994), *Guidelines on Advocacy for Mental Health Workers*, London: Unison.
Sang, B. and O'Brien, J. (1989), *Advocacy: The UK and American Experiences*, Kings Fund Project, Paper No. 51, London.
Sherr, A. (1993), *Advocacy*, London: Blackstone Press.

Assertiveness

Bach, K. and Bach, K. (1982), *Assertiveness at Work*, London: McGraw-Hill.
Dickson, A. (1982), *A Woman in Your Own Right*, London: Quartet.
Galassi, M. D. and Galassi, J. P. (1977), *Assert Yourself*, New York: Human Sciences Press.
Kelley, C. (1979), *Assertion Training*, San Diego: University Associates.
Sundel, S. S. and Sundel, M. (1980), *Be Assertive*, Beverley Hills: Sage.

Negotiation

Fisher, R. and Ury, W. (1986), *Getting to Yes – Negotiating Agreement Without Giving In*, London: Hutchinson.

Gold, N., Mackie, K. and Twining, W. (1989), *Learning Lawyers Skills*, London: Butterworth.

Time management

Adair, J. (1989), *Effective Time Management*, London: Pan.
Blanchard, K. and Spencer, J. (1983), *The One Minute Manager*, London: Fontana. (A series of books about the One Minute Manager have also been published.)
Garratt, S. (1985), Manage Your Time, London: Fontana/Collins.
Noon, J. (1983), *Time for Success*, London: International Thompson.
Noon, J. (1985), *'A' Time*, London: Chapman and Hall.

Stress management

Arroba, T. and James, K. (1987), *Pressure at Work*, London: McGraw-Hill.
Madden, J. (1979), *Stress and Relaxation*, London: Martin Dunitz.
Patel, C. (1989), *The Complete Guide to Stress Management*, London: Optima.

Basic reference books on welfare law

These are annual publications unless stated otherwise so you should always use the latest edition.

Arden, A. and Hunter, C. (1993), *Manual of Housing Law*, London: Sweet & Maxwell.
Benefits: CHAR's guide to means-tested benefits for single people without a permanent home, London: Campaign for the Homeless and Rootless.
Bonner, D., Hooker, I. and White, R., *Non-Means-Tested Benefits: The Legislation*, London: Sweet & Maxwell.
Child Support Handbook, London: Child Poverty Action Group.
Cooper, J. (1994), *The Legal Rights Manual* (2nd edn), Aldershot: Arena.
Disability Rights Handbook, London: Disability Alliance.
Encyclopaedia of Social Services Law, London: Butterworth.
Findlay, L. and Ward, M., *CPAG's Housing Benefit and Council Tax Benefit Legislation*, London: Child Poverty Action Group.
Forbes, D. and Madge, N. (1993), *Debt and Housing Emergency Procedures*, London: Legal Action Group.
Gray, J. (1992), *A Guide to Money Advice in Scotland*, London: Child Poverty Action Group.
Hoffland, A. and Nicol, N., *Fuel Rights Handbook*, London: Child Poverty Action Group.
Homelessness Code of Guidance (1989), London: HMSO.

Hunter, C. and McGrath, S. (1994), *Homeless Persons*, London: Legal Action Group.

Jacobs, E. and Douglas, G., *Child Support: The Legislation*, London: Sweet & Maxwell.

Luba, J., Madge, N. and McConnell, D. (1993), *Defending Possession Proceedings*, London: Legal Action Group.

McKenny, J. and Thompson, L., *Rights Guide for Home Owners*, London: Child Poverty Action Group.

Mesher, J., *CPAG's Income-Related Benefits: The Legislation*, London: Sweet & Maxwell.

Morris, P., Rahal, I., Storey, H. and Gurney, J. (1993), *Ethnic Minorities' Benefits Handbook*, London: Child Poverty Action Group.

National Welfare Benefits Handbook, London: Child Poverty Action Group.

Randall, G. (1992), Housing Rights Guide, London: Shac.

Rights Guide to Non-means-Tested Benefits, London: Child Poverty Action Group.

Rowland, M., *Medical and Disability Appeal Tribunals: The Legislation*, London: Sweet & Maxwell.

Ward, M. (1993), *Council Tax Handbook*, London: Child Poverty Action Group.

Ward, M. and Zebedee, J., *A Guide to Housing Benefit and Council Tax Benefit*, London: Ioh/Shac.

Wolfe, M. and Ivison, J. (1993), *Debt Advice Handbook*, London: Child Poverty Action Group.

Index

— The —
LEGAL RIGHTS
Manual

SECOND EDITION

A guide for social workers and advice centres

Jeremy Cooper

This book provides social workers, advice centres and those engaged in caring for others, together with their clients, with an up-to-date body of information and advice on their legal rights, covering a wide range of areas and activities.

Written in a concise, non-technical and readable style the book describes how individuals and groups can use the law to their advantage in a diverse range of settings, including: housing, the workplace; living with mental or physical disability, dealing with council and other public officials, problems with the police, living with old age, and as a consumer of goods and services. It also provides the reader with a mass of information on where to go for further advice and assistance in each of these areas. This fully updated and revised second edition states the law as it stands on 1 March 1994.

Jeremy Cooper is a barrister and Professor of Law and Head of the Law Division at the Southampton Institute.

1994   319 pages   1 85742 136 1   £19.95

Price subject to change without notification

arena

The Children
Act *1989:*
Putting it into Practice
Mary Ryan

This book provides a practical guide to those parts of the Children Act 1989 that relate to the provision of services by local authorities to children and families; the powers and duties of local authorities in such circumstances; care and supervision proceedings; and child protection issues.

The book is a unique combination of information on the legal framework contained in the Act, regulations and guidance and information on good social work and legal practice, relevant research and recent case law. It is grounded on the author's practical experience of providing an advice and advocacy service for families; providing training for social workers, lawyers and other child care professionals; being involved with the development of the legislation from the consultation period in the early 1980s, through the parliamentary process, and the subsequent consultation on regulations, guidance and court rules.

Mary Ryan, the Co-Director of the Family Rights Group, is a solicitor who after working in private practice as a family lawyer, was the Family Rights Group's legal advisor for 10 years.

1994   256 pages

Hbk   1 85742 192 2   £30.00   Pbk   1 85742 193 0   £14.95

Price subject to change without notification

arena

GROUPWORK

3rd Edition
Allan Brown

"If required to recommend just one book on working with groups, this would always be the choice" **Community Care**

"Allan Brown's book has made its mark by its overall balanced view, its accessible style, and, let us spell it out: at a price that front line low paid workers can afford. It offers up-to-date groupwork knowledge relevant to the harsh reality of front line practice. Third time round; it does it again with increased breadth." **British Journal of Social Work**

This highly successful book on groupwork practice, first published in 1979, has become a standard introductory text on most social work training courses. It is very popular with social workers, whatever their agency setting, and is also used by health visitors, youth workers and the voluntary sector.

This enlarged and revised third edition includes two new additional chapters. The first of these addresses the issue of groupwork in day and residential centres where special kinds of group skills are required in addition to those already well established for fieldwork groups. The second new chapter attempts to understand the significance of race and gender in groupwork and to begin to develop a framework for anti-discriminatory practice.

Allan Brown is Senior Lecturer in Social Work at Bristol University.

1992   239 pages   1 85742 087 X   £8.99

Price subject to change without notification

Personal Safety for Social Workers

Pauline Bibby

Commissioned by
The Suzy Lamplugh Trust
Foreword by
Diana Lamplugh OBE

This book is aimed at employers, managers and staff in social work agencies.

In part 1, *Personal Safety for Social Workers* deals with the respective roles and responsibilities of employers and employees are discussed, and offers guidance on developing a workplace personal safety policy. The design and management of the workplace are considered and guidelines provided for social workers working away from the normal work base. Part 2 contains detailed guidelines for use by individual social workers in a variety of work situations. Part 3 addresses training issues and provides a number of sample training programmes.

The message of this book is that proper attention to risk can reduce both the incidence of aggression and its development into violent acts.

1994   224 pages   1 85742 195 7   £16.95

Price subject to change without notification

arena

LIMA TECHNICAL COLLEGE
LIMA CAMPUS LIBRARY

CONCISE GUIDE TO

Customs of Minority Ethnic Religions

David Collins
Manju Tank
Abdul Basith

Much has been written on the subject of Community Relations. This small book does not claim to add to this knowledge, but rather to distil it in a brief, orderly, and accessible form for the everyday reader, who needs basic guidance for the purposes of everyday work. It makes no assumptions about existing understanding or interest on the part of the reader, and aims to enable readers to meet the needs of minority ethnic consumers in a more sensitive and respectful way.

The Guide contains basic useful information on Judaism, Sikhism, Hinduism, Islam, Buddhism/Taoism/Confucianism, and Rastafarianism. Each section is divided into modules dealing with Symbols, Languages and Scripts, Names, Beliefs, Prayer, Religious Festivals, Dress, Diet, Medical Treatment, Social Rules, Birth Customs and Visiting.

1993   84 pages   1 85742 120 5   £5.50

Price subject to change without notification

arena